Apostolic Mindsets & Paradigms

Understanding the Apostolic Ministry

By

Tonderai Mupamhanga

FOREWORD BY APOSTLE COLIN NYATHI

Apostolic Mindsets & Paradigms

Copyright © 2014 by Tonderai Mupamhanga

ISBN 978-0-7974-9496-1

Design & Typeset:

Inkdrops Publishing

Dedication

To the Harvest House International Church family, serving God in this house has never been better or sweeter. With more than a decade of serving Him in Harvest House International, it gets better and better every day. I am grateful to be part of such a great Apostolic Ministry.

Acknowledgments

To Apostles Colin & Sarah Nyathi, ministry and life has never been the same for me since I joined Harvest House International. It is an absolute joy, pleasure and honour to be an apostolic son serving under you. Thank you for allowing me to discover and express the call of God upon my life through your guidance and ministry.

To Bishops C.S. & N. Tuturu, the mentoring, training, teaching and grooming in my life could never have been better. What amazing inputs and deposits that you placed in me. I will always value and cherish you.

To my one and only beautiful wife Patience and my two beloved children, Anotida and Atida, you are all amazing. You bring joy to my life daily. And to my father, Nephtal Mupamhanga and my late mother Sylvia Mupamhanga, thank you for the sober habits and stability that you brought into my life.

Foreword

It is always important for the church to be spiritually alert and aware prophetically. This is a time when the Holy Spirit is making the Body of Christ aware of its apostolic nature and calling. Clear teaching is needed so as to propel God's strategies that will enable the apostolic anointing for the spiritual awakening that God promised and for which He is preparing His church.

Yes the harvest is imminent and more and more Christians are aware of this. However, the church has to be ready for such a time. Multitudes will be in the valley of decision and when they start to recognize the Lordship of Jesus Christ and there will be a sudden and great influx of people into the church. For this the church has to prepare.

In recent decades, we have witnessed a restoration of the teaching, evangelistic and prophetic ministries. New believers have to recognize the need for apostolic mindsets and paradigms as well as apostolic covering in the right sense.

For in recent years there have been many who claim to be apostles but are not because their ministries do not measure up to the biblical description of the ministry of an Apostle. And there have been several non-biblical concepts of apostolic covering that have resulted in people lording it over others instead of leading, enabling and equipping through example the obvious anointing on their lives.

When a person is a true apostle, he is recognized as such by others without having to make extravagant claims for himself.

This teaching by Bishop Tonderai Mupamhanga on the Apostolic Call and Vision, Apostolic Maturity, Apostolic Mindsets and Paradigm Shifts for churches and leaders is a clear biblical teaching that brings forth the true nature of the apostolic ministry and how this needs to pervade the structure of the whole body of Christ.

I trust that this book, "Apostolic Mindsets and Paradigms" will help the church to understand God's purpose apostolically, and to take steps to see that this teaching is implemented.

Apostle Colin Nyathi
Founder & Senior Pastor
Harvest House International

Table of Contents

Chapter One: The Apostolic Call And Vision

Introduction

The advent of an apostolic call and vision is the beginning of an exciting and yet challenging journey to greatness. Nothing drives the purposes and plans of God for His church and His people more than an apostolic vision. A God given vision tends to move swiftly and expeditiously when it is propelled by the apostolic dimension. There are many kinds of visions that people receive and run with, however, an apostolic vision is distinctly unique and exceptional. In fact many other visions can only find expression within the context of a greater apostolic vision.

Anyone who wants to succeed in leadership and ministry should fully embrace apostolic dynamics and apply apostolic principles. It is absolutely crucial to understand that great exploits are born through the release and execution of apostolic visions.

People who receive, embrace and implement apostolic visions always emerge as people of great exploits. Every great story in the Kingdom of God is founded in the release of an apostolic call and vision. Building on the foundation of an apostolic call and vision is critical to the success of anyone who desires to work for God.

Ephesians 2:20 - *"And are built upon the foundation of the apostles and prophets, Jesus Christ himself being the chief corner stone..."*

In the Bible, there are several men and women who received great apostolic visions and assignments from God. It was through their acceptance and assumption of these that they managed to achieve great things. These exploits were done by people who were sent by God with a specific mandate.

Isaiah 61:1-11 - *"The Spirit of the Lord GOD is upon me; because the LORD hath anointed me to preach good tidings unto the meek; he hath sent me to bind up the broken - hearted, to proclaim liberty to the captives, and the opening of the prison to them that are bound; To proclaim the acceptable year of the LORD, and the day of vengeance of our God; to comfort all that mourn; To appoint unto them that mourn in Zion, to give unto them beauty for ashes, the oil of joy for mourning, the garment of praise for the spirit of heaviness; that they might be called trees of righteousness, the planting of the LORD, that he might be glorified"*

The Scripture above refers to the Lord Jesus Christ who was sent and anointed by God to execute an apostolic vision that changed the destiny of mankind. Everyone who believes in the Lord Jesus Christ and receives Him will be able to experience everything that is contained in this apostolic vision.

Biblical Examples of Apostolic Visions & Callings

1. The Calling of Abraham

Abraham received an apostolic call and mandate from God in the book of Genesis.

Genesis 12:1–3 - *"Now the LORD had said unto Abram, Get thee out of thy country, and from thy kindred, and from thy father's house, unto a land that I will show thee: And I will make of thee a great nation, and I will bless thee, and make thy name great; and thou shalt be a blessing. And I will bless them that bless thee, and curse him that curseth thee: and in thee shall all families of the earth be blessed. "*

Abraham responded positively to this apostolic call and vision. It was a vision that would change his entire life as he began a journey into the apostolic.

Genesis 12:4 - *"So Abram departed, as the LORD had spoken unto him; and Lot went with him: and Abram was seventy and five years old when he departed out of Haran."*

Today, children of God are all blessed through the father of faith Abraham because he obeyed the apostolic call by God upon his life.

Galatians 3:7 - *"Know ye therefore, that they who are of faith, the same are the children of Abraham."*
There are always blessings contained within every apostolic vision or assignment. These blessings are released to those who diligently obey and hook onto the apostolic vision.

2. The Calling of Moses
Moses also received an apostolic call and vision from God in the book of Exodus.

Exodus 3:10 - *"Come now therefore, and I will send thee unto Pharaoh, that thou mayest bring* *forth my people the children of Israel out of Egypt."*

After debating with God about this apostolic vision, Moses eventually decided to follow the call of God upon his life. When he made a step into this vision, amazing experiences followed his life. Moses performed many signs in Egypt and became a very great man amongst the people.

Exodus 11:3 - *"And the LORD gave the people favour in the sight of the Egyptians. Moreover the man Moses was very great in the land of Egypt, in the sight of Pharaoh's servants, and in the sight of the people"*

Exodus 4:30 - *"And Aaron spoke all the words which the LORD had spoken to Moses, and performed the signs in the sight of the people."*

The favour of the Lord, signs, wonders and greatness follow those who are hooked onto an apostolic vision. It is through obedience to such an apostolic vision that Moses was lifted up greatly.

3. The Calling of Samuel

Samuel received an apostolic vision from God concerning the nation of Israel in the book of Samuel.

1 Samuel 3:10 - *"And the LORD came, and stood, and called as at other times, Samuel, Samuel. Then Samuel answered, Speak, for thy servant heareth."*

1 Samuel 3:11 - *"And the LORD said to Samuel, Behold, I will do a thing in Israel, at which both the ears of every one that heareth it shall tingle."*

When God placed an apostolic vision into the heart of Samuel, he took heed to the voice of the Lord. From that time onwards, Samuel began to rise as a great man of God in Israel.

1 Samuel 3:19–20 -*"And Samuel grew, and the LORD was with him, and did let none of his words fall to the ground. And all Israel from Dan even to Beersheba knew that Samuel was established to be a prophet of the LORD."*

Samuel became a very powerful force in the land of Israel. His life influenced the affairs of an entire nation. His apostolic and prophetic ministry was well established in the land of Israel. All the people in Israel knew Samuel as a genuine man of God.

1 Samuel 7:13 - *"So the Philistines were subdued, and they came no more into the coast of Israel: and the hand of the LORD was against the Philistines all the days of Samuel."*

1 Samuel 7:15 - *"And Samuel judged Israel all the days of his life."*

During the tenure of Samuel as a judge, the Philistines were subdued because of his apostolic influence over the land.

4. The Calling of John the Baptist

John the Baptist also received an apostolic vision as a forerunner to the coming of Christ. He was sent from God with a clear divine mandate on his life.

John 1:6 - *"There was a man sent from God, whose name was John."*

John 1:23 - *"He said, I am the voice of one crying in the wilderness, Make straight the way of the Lord, as said the prophet Esaias."*

The ministry of John the Baptist shook the nation of Israel as people of all backgrounds gathered around him.

John 1:19 - *"And this is the testimony of John, when the Jews sent priests and Levites from Jerusalem, to ask him, Who art thou?"*

Tax collectors, solders, Pharisees, Levites and priests were all affected by his ministry. He had such an impact on the nation such that many actually thought that he was the Messiah. The apostolic call is so powerful such people automatically hook themselves to an apostolic leader because of influential nature of the apostolic.

5. The Calling of Paul

When Paul met God, there was a deposit of an apostolic call and vision that took place in his life. His life was never the same again after his encounter with the Lord Jesus Christ.

Acts 9:4, 6 - *"And he fell to the earth, and heard a voice saying unto him, Saul, Saul, why persecutest thou me? And he trembling and astonished said, Lord, what wilt thou have me to* *do? And the Lord said unto him, Arise, and go into the city, and it shall be told thee what thou must do."*

When Paul received this apostolic vision, a radical transformation took place in his life. He became a man of great exploits through the deposit of this apostolic vision. His apostolic ministry was so powerful such that he made a mark for God everywhere he went.

Acts 14:11 - *"And when the people saw what Paul had done, they lifted up their voices, saying in the speech of Lycaonia, The gods are come down to us in the likeness of men."*

Paul rose up to become one of the greatest Apostles of his time with amazing levels of revelation, grace, signs and wonders following him.

Emotional Excitement vs Genuine Apostolic Vision

There are people who confuse emotional excitement for a genuine apostolic call or vision. There are many reasons why people get excited and in the process, make the mistake that such feelings indicate an apostolic calling. There are some who see God using them in an amazing way and immediately assume that it's an indication that God is calling them to launch an apostolic ministry.

There are also some who are deceived by the crowds that enjoy their preaching or ministry. These wrongly interpret the occurrence to be an endorsement to start churches or ministries. There is also a wrong and erroneous notion that says 'to be apostolic means starting a new work, church or ministry'. This will be addressed in more detail later in this book.

It is important to note that peculiar spiritual experiences and the accompanying excitement that comes with it should not be misconstrued or misinterpreted to mean that God is calling someone into the apostolic office. Some people often get big-headed after a few accomplishments in ministry and run away from God ordained apostolic structures to start their own ministries and churches.

There are many who have claimed to have received an apostolic vision and embarked on the journey but closed shop after realizing their mistakes. No matter the level of spiritual excitement that one gets, God does not approve or sanction something that He has not ordained. Claiming to be an apostle or prophet does not make one an apostle or a prophet. It certainly does not mean anything to claim titles if God has not called someone.

Young ministers should be careful not to run into things that they do not fully understand. A lot of ministers who had a genuine call of God upon them have ruined their destinies because of the excitement and failure to perceive divine things. It is easy to run on excitement or an emotional tangent and totally miss God in the process. Unfortunately the call of God is not about emotions or excitement, because it cannot be sustained by emotions. Many find it very hard to push what they started when emotions have died down. This is because God was never involved in the first place.

Defining an Apostolic Vision

An Apostolic Vision is a God-ordained and transformational type vision which God communicates to individuals with the intention of fulfilling His eternal purposes as well as expanding His Kingdom.

It is crucial to note that an apostolic vision is a crystal clear mandate that God delivers to His chosen vessels. This mandate has the power to transform societies, cities and nations.

Characteristics of an Apostolic Vision

1. It is a heavenly vision

Every genuine apostolic vision is divine and born from heaven. God is the author of every kind of Apostolic Vision.

Acts 26:19 - *"Whereupon, O king Agrippa, I was not disobedient unto the heavenly vision."*

Apostolic visions are birthed from heaven. A man with an apostolic vision is sent from God. **John 1:6** - *"There was a man sent from God, whose name was John."*

There are many people who think that they can run with an apostolic vision in their own power. The end result of anything which is not authored by God is frustration. Not every good idea is a God idea. There are so many

15

assignments that some ministers do without the hand of God upon them. This always ends up in disappointment because God was never involved in the assignment from the very onset.

Whilst it is easy for any Jack and Jill to claim that they are called to lead an apostolic vision or pioneer an apostolic work, it is only those that are genuinely called by God that will succeed. Many are called to hook onto an apostolic vision and serve under that apostolic vision. Serving under an apostolic vision opens many doors and opportunities for individuals who are genuine.

Habakkuk 2:2 - *"And the LORD answered me, and said, Write the vision, and make it plain upon tables, that he may run that readeth it."*

For any vision to succeed it should have its roots in God. Genuine ministers are those that carry visions that are birthed from heaven. Fleshly and earthly visions do not last long. All the great men of God who succeeded in their destinies had received the vision from God.

2. It is a destiny vision

Every apostolic vision is a vision of destiny. It launches men and women into their destinies. Moses was launched into his destiny through the apostolic vision that he received from God. Paul was propelled into his destiny through the apostolic vision that he received from God. Apostolic visions have a way of driving men and women towards their God given purposes.

Philippians 3:13-14 - *"Brethren, I count not myself to have apprehended: but this one thing I do , forgetting those things which are behind, and reaching forth unto those things which are before, I press toward the mark for the prize of the high calling of God in Christ Jesus."*

Anyone who embraces an apostolic vision will always push for something higher. The nature of any genuine apostolic vision is that it drives people into seeking higher levels in God.

17

2 Timothy 4:7 - *"I have fought a good fight, I have finished my course, I have kept the faith."*

Apostolic visions always define and unravel the destinies of people. Anyone who desires to find his or her destiny should hook onto an apostolic vision. There are many people who spent all their lives seeking to find purpose and meaning to their lives without success. We are living in a world where many people are yearning to find fulfillment and meaning to life. There is a general sense of frustration and emptiness that often disturbs many people as they seek to reach the place of fulfillment.

One of the greatest keys to finding purpose and vision is to connect to a dynamic apostolic vision. It is through submitting and serving under that vision that the sense of direction and destiny begins to grow.

Jeremiah 1:5 - *"Before I formed thee in the belly I knew thee; and before thou camest forth* *out of the womb I sanctified thee, and I ordained thee a prophet unto the nations."*

Galatians 1:15 - *"But when it pleased God, who separated me from my mother's womb, and called me by his grace."*

Hebrews 10:7 - *"Then said I, Lo, I come (in the volume of the book it is written of me,) to do thy will, O God."*

The children of Israel found their destiny and deliverance through the apostolic and prophetic ministry of Moses.

Hosea 12:13 - *"And by a prophet the LORD brought Israel out of Egypt, and by a prophet was he preserved."*

Any serious individual who desires to be used by God will hook onto an apostolic vision to find their destiny. It is absolutely important to listen to the call of destiny and desire to see the full

19

manifestation of that destiny. A genuine apostolic vision equips everyone who desires to follow that path with grace and tools to fulfill destiny.

3. It is a Generational Vision

Apostolic visions are generational in nature. This means that any authentic apostolic vision has a generational impact. The Apostolic Vision that Abraham received affected many generations after him. It continues to affect generations even up to-date.

Isaiah 51:2 - *"Look unto Abraham your father, and unto Sarah that bare you: for I called him alone, and blessed him, and increased him."*

Galatians 3:13-14 - *"Christ hath redeemed us from the curse of the law, being made a curse for us: for it is written, Cursed is every one that hangeth on a tree: That the blessing of Abraham might come on the Gentiles through Jesus Christ;*

that we might receive the promise of the Spirit through faith."

Any apostolic vision will outlive the people that originally received and embraced it. There is need for leaders to be generational visionaries and generational thinkers for them to perpetuate an apostolic vision.

4. It is a Pioneering Vision
An apostolic vision comes with a pioneering spirit. There are things that become easy to do because of what is released from an apostolic vision. Apostolic visions open up new avenues and prepare a way for others. There is a ground-breaking spirit that comes upon people who are connected to an apostolic vision.

There are things that are yet to be seen in this generation because of the apostolic spirit that God is releasing upon the church. Moses opened up the way for the children of Israel through the apostolic vision that he received

21

from God. There are territories that the church is yet to occupy.

5. It is a Transformational Vision

Apostolic visions always cause great transformations to people, generations, cities and nations. People who receive and participate actively in an apostolic vision are continuously transformed from glory to glory.

Paul was totally transformed when he received an apostolic vision from God. In as much as he had previously persecuted the church, when he received this vision through a divine encounter with the Lord Jesus, it caused a radical shift in his life.

Acts 9:4, 6 -*"And he fell to the earth, and heard a voice saying unto him, Saul, Saul, why persecutest thou me? And he trembling and astonished said, Lord, what wilt thou have me to do? And the Lord said unto him, Arise, and go* *into the city, and it shall be told thee what thou must do."*

His ministry was also highly apostolic and hence his impact as a minister of God's word transformed multitudes of people. Wherever Paul went, there were amazing transformational changes that took place in the lives of the people.

Acts 17:6 - *"And when they found them not, they drew Jason and certain brethren unto the rulers of the city, crying, These that have turned the world upside down are come hither also"*

In the days of Samuel, the nation of Israel was never the same after God had raised Samuel. Therefore, whenever God releases an apostolic vision, transformation is inevitable.

6. It is a Directional Vision

Apostolic visions are directional visions. They reveal the way forward or the direction which people should follow and should take. Divine direction becomes very clear through apostolic visions.

Acts 13:2 - *"As they ministered to the Lord, and fasted, the Holy Ghost said, Separate me Barnabas and Saul for the work whereunto I have called them."*

People that carry apostolic visions are people of direction. When we begin to embrace apostolic vision, our lives become full of direction.

Isaiah 30:21 - *"And thine ears shall hear a word behind thee, saying, This is the way, walk ye in it, when ye turn to the right hand, and when ye turn to the left."*

7. It is a Progressive Vision

Apostolic visions are visions that advance God's kingdom. Every apostolic vision sees opportunity to invade new territories. People that carry an apostolic vision have an appetite to break new ground and be progressive. What guarantees progress in life is the apostolic spirit that one carries. So an apostolic vision both advances the Kingdom of God at the same time causes progress in the lives of those that are connected to it.

Matthew 11:12 - *"And from the days of John the Baptist until now the kingdom of heaven suffereth violence, and the violent take it by force."*

Many people begin to make significant progress in their lives once they start living the apostolic lifestyle. This is a lifestyle that is sold out to the cause of an apostolic vision which is in line with the purposes and plans of God. People who serve, give and sacrifice their lives to the cause of an apostolic vision make great strides and progress in life.

There are numerous people who desire to make progress in life but the problem is that they do not belong anywhere. Anyone who does not get into the programs and purposes of God has limited chances of making any meaningful headway and progress in life. There are some who prefer to take a spectator approach to divine things and in the process they miss out on the best that God has in store for them.

Benefits of carrying an Apostolic Vision

1. Divine Guidance

God always guides those who align to His purposes and plans. One of the best ways of being in the purposes of God is by aligning to an apostolic vision.

Isaiah 45:2 - *"I will go before thee, and make the crooked places straight: I will break in pieces the gates of brass, and cut in sunder the bars of iron"*

People who carry apostolic visions are always guaranteed that God will go before them.

Psalm 24:7 - *"Lift up your heads, O ye gates; and be ye lift up, ye everlasting doors; and the King of glory shall come in."*

When one carries or lines up with an apostolic vision, they are guaranteed that certain doors will automatically be opened for them. Abraham continued to enjoy divine guidance throughout his life through embracing and aligning with an apostolic vision that God had given him.

2. Divine Protection

When a church aligns to an apostolic vision, the people of God are protected by God.

Psalm 121:4 - *"Behold, he that keepeth Israel shall neither slumber nor sleep."*

Psalm 121:5-6 - *"The LORD is thy keeper: the LORD is thy shade upon thy right hand. The sun shall not smite thee by day, nor the moon by night"*

God protects those who keep in line with His plans and purposes.

3. Divine Partnership

Every person who embraces and runs with an apostolic vision from God is guaranteed of divine partnership.

Mark 16:20 - *"And they went forth, and preached everywhere, the Lord working with them, and confirming the word with signs following."*

Divine Partnership is when God partners with his people in the work. In any situation God stands with those that carry this vision because of the importance of the vision in God's mind.

4. Divine Grace

There is a special grace that flows within every apostolic vision. Grace is the measure of ability and favour that God gives in order for one to operate in a unique way. God supplies grace to those that are aligned to an apostolic vision.

1Corinthians 15:10 - *"But by the grace of God I am what I am: and his grace which was bestowed upon me was not in vain; but I laboured more abundantly than they all: yet not I, but the grace of God which was with me."*

Grace is also the measure of how far one can do certain tasks in God's kingdom. We all need grace to excel in the kingdom of God.

5. Divine Covering

An Apostolic Vision also comes with divine covering. People who embrace and flow with an apostolic vision have a special divine covering over their lives. Some people operate without divine covering because they do not belong to any apostolic vision or structure. When one walks out of God-ordained structures they become vulnerable. God has ordained apostolic visions and structures as places for covering.

The nation of Israel was covered and safe from the attacks of the Philistines during the days of Prophet Samuel. There was a special hand of God that was upon the entire nation such that the Philistines were subdued and did not come into the territory of Israel. It is important for every believer to function within proper God-ordained apostolic structures to find divine covering.

1 Samuel 7:13 - *"So the Philistines were subdued, and they came no more into the coast of Israel: and the hand of the LORD was against the Philistines all the days of Samuel."*

The children of Israel were also covered under the apostolic ministry of Moses. There was a cloud that followed them as they crossed the Red Sea and journeyed in the wilderness.

1 Corinthians 10:1-2 - *"Moreover, brethren, I would not that ye should be ignorant, how that all our fathers were under the cloud, and all passed through the sea; And were all baptized unto Moses in the cloud and in the sea."*

This cloud was a special covering that God provided because of the apostolic structure that He had put in place. In the Body of Christ today, there are several people who have chosen to go solo and consequently despise all forms of covering. Many of them have been hurt along the way in ministry and some have ruined their destinies.

Apostolic Mindsets & Paradigms

Chapter Two: Apostolic Maturity Process

Ephesians 4:11-14 - *"And he gave some, apostles; and some, prophets; and some, evangelists; and some, pastors and teachers; For the perfecting of the saints, for the work of the ministry, for the edifying of the body of Christ: Till we all come in the unity of the faith, and of the knowledge of the Son of God, unto a perfect man, unto the measure of the stature of the fullness of Christ: That we henceforth be no more children, tossed to and fro, and carried about with every wind of doctrine, by the sleight of men, and cunning craftiness, whereby they lie in wait to deceive."*

In order to understand the Apostolic Maturity Process, it is essential to firstly understand that there are several categories of apostolic people that exist or function within an apostolic structure or vision.

33

Apostolic Categories

There are diverse classes of people that operate within an Apostolic Vision or Structure.

The Word **'Apostle'** means an ambassador, a messenger or one that is sent. This means that the term **'Apostolic'** has to do with being sent on a mission.

To begin with, all believers are sent people in the sense that God has sent them to reach out to the world with the Gospel of Christ. If believers possess this sent mentality it means that they are apostolic people in a way. It is important therefore, to exhibit an apostolic perspective and mentality that is oriented towards fulfilling God's purposes on earth. This way, believers can carry an apostolic spirit that can cause them to do great exploits for God.

However, is it key to note that not all believers are called to be **'Apostles'**. The office of the

Apostle is a special calling that God gives to those that He chooses to lead or to pioneer Apostolic Visions, Churches or Movements. Many believers therefore only operate within an apostolic vision that is founded or led by an apostle. They function as apostolic sons in an apostolic vision. Some of them may be leaders who are called to the five-fold ministry e.g. Pastors, Evangelists, Prophets and Teachers, or Elders. Some of them may be leaders that function as Deacons e.g. worship leaders, departmental leaders or ministry workers. And some may just be ordinary people serving under an Apostle or an Apostolic Vision.

Crisis begins when those that are called to serve under an apostolic structure also claim that they are called to be 'Apostles'. There are several people who have taken this route without being called by God into the office of the Apostle. The challenge is that these individuals never really excel and rise up to their full potential because they are out of place. When people are out of the place that God has ordained for them, they will struggle to serve God effectively because they do not have the divine authority to make any meaningful impact. It is important therefore for believers to submit to an apostolic ministry or an Apostle that can raise them and propel them to their fullest potential.

Defining Apostolic Maturity

Apostolic Maturity refers to the development of the apostolic spirit or ministry in an individual or church such that the individual or the church begins to exhibit clear apostolic qualities that are evident to society.

The Apostolic spirit or ministry grows within individuals or churches overtime. As the apostolic ministry matures and develops, the authority of the church or individuals also grows. All believers can grow the apostolic spirit in them especially as they serve under a genuine apostolic ministry.

Apostolic maturity will manifest through the release of a powerful, dominant and governing anointing that begins to flow through the individual or the church. This anointing is not limited to a small group of people but it usually influences an entire location, village, city, nation or even nations.

Maturity Levels of Churches

It is crucial for individuals and leaders in the Body of Christ to understand the maturity levels of churches as they seek to build the church and take it to higher levels. These are stages that churches normally go through as they move to higher dimensions of ministry. Churches, institutions and organizations go through various stages and maturity levels of development. Leaders should therefore understand the maturity level of their churches or the various portfolios they lead within the church. In the same way that individuals mature spiritually, churches also mature overtime. God has placed the five-fold ministry gifts in the Body of Christ to usher the church into higher levels of maturity and perfection.

Ephesians 4:11–14 - *"And he gave some, apostles; and some, prophets; and some, evangelists; and some, pastors and teachers; For the perfecting of the saints, for the work of the ministry, for the edifying of the body of Christ: Till we all come in the unity of the faith, and of the knowledge of the Son of God, unto a perfect man, unto the measure of the stature of the fullness of Christ: That we henceforth be no more children, tossed to and fro, and carried about with every wind of doctrine, by the sleight of men, and cunning craftiness, whereby they lie in wait to deceive."*

The Scripture above clearly states that the reason why the five-fold ministers i.e. **Apostles,**

Prophets, Evangelists, Pastors and Teachers were given to the Body of Christ was to ensure that the church matures, increases in the knowledge of Christ and grows in stature. This means that pastors and ministers in the church need to work on maturing the church from one level of maturity to another. It should be the joy of every Christian leader to see the church maturing and developing overtime. Understanding the maturity level of the church then helps leaders to put in place systems and structures that are meant to take the church higher.

The Process of Maturity

The maturity of the church is not something that happens overnight. Many leaders and ministers get frustrated when they do not see instant changes in their churches or ministries. After much effort in counseling, teaching, preaching and training some ministers get discouraged because the church will not be maturing at the rate they expect. It takes time and effort to develop the maturity levels of a church and the departments that function within that church. Leaders have to be prepared to work extra hard and go the extra mile before they can see the desired changes.

The church at Corinth was still at a very low maturity level and Paul had to teach and impart certain things unto them. The church was still struggling with issues of sin, divisions, fighting and general governance.

1 Corinthians 3:1 - *"And I, brethren, could not speak unto you as unto spiritual, but as unto carnal, even as unto babes in Christ."*

Paul wrote two letters to this church trying to explain how they were supposed to handle issues that they were struggling with. He also dedicates these letters, explaining how they ought to administer church affairs, public ministry and many other social issues.

The writer to the Book of Hebrews also noticed that the church was not growing and maturing at the level which was expected.

Hebrews 5:12 - *"For when for the time ye ought to be teachers, ye have need that one teach you again which be the first principles of the oracles of God; and are become such as have need of milk, and not of strong meat."*

These saints were generally lower in maturity than expected. The expectation was for the church to be at the level of being teachers but they still needed to be taught. This tends to be the dilemma of many leaders because of the way they perceive and project growth and maturity in their churches.

The church in Galatia also faced a similar challenge. Paul was not amused by the way the church was being misled and falling into different kinds of deception.

Galatians 1:6–8 - *"I marvel that ye are so soon removed from him that called you into the grace of Christ unto another gospel: Which is not another; but there be some that trouble you, and would pervert the gospel of Christ. But though we, or an angel from heaven, preach any other gospel unto you than that which we have preached unto you, let him be accursed."*

Galatians 4:19 - *"My little children, of whom I travail in birth again until Christ be formed in you..."*

One of the greatest challenges of a church that does not mature is that it is vulnerable to lots of deception. This was exactly the case with the Galatian church. In recent times, several churches have lost members as a result of the rise of false prophets and teachers who have risen with very deceptive teachings. This has caused a number of immature believers to leave their churches. Immature believers tend to focus on the spectacular presentation of the Gospel more than real doctrine.

On the other hand, when believers and churches are mature, they are not easily shaken or deceived. They remain solid and steadfast in the faith despite the rise of all manner of winds as doctrine and deceptive spirits. The maturity of the church will also increase its effectiveness, relevance and impact. God desires and is calling churches to grow and mature so that they can influence societies.

Maturity Factors

The maturity and strength of an organisation or church depends on three primary factors:

1. The Quality of the Word (Information)
The quality of the word, information and training material given to the people determines the maturity level of a church. Without consistent teaching of God's Word, ministry

principles and values the church will not mature. It is therefore crucial for leaders to carefully choose and select what they give in terms of the Word so as to strengthen the people of God and the church at large.

If leaders preach or teach a low quality Word they will also produce low quality people. Practical issues of life should also be addressed to ensure that the church remains well informed on a wide range of matters that affect its stability. A church that is not well informed will suffer from instability.

Hosea 4:6 - *"My people are destroyed for lack of knowledge: because thou hast rejected knowledge, I will also reject thee, that thou shalt be no priest to me: seeing thou hast forgotten the law of thy God, I will also forget thy children."*

The lack of knowledge and ignorance brings destruction. The church at Corinth was negatively affected in maturity because of its ignorance on many issues.

1 Corinthians 12:1 - *"Now concerning spiritual gifts, brethren, I would not have you ignorant."*

Ignorance is the greatest enemy to the maturity of individuals and churches. Pastors and ministers should be careful not just to have meetings, but be very mindful of the quality of the word, information given as well as training offered to people. There must be a deliberate effort to have long term plans on issues that need to be emphasized and addressed in a church. These are efforts that should be oriented towards equipping the church with quality information and the sound word of God.

2 Timothy 2:2 - *"And the things that thou hast heard of me among many witnesses, the same commit thou to faithful men, who shall be able to teach others also."*

Paul here encouraged Timothy to commit the things he had learnt to faithful people who would also further teach others. When information and sound teachings are cascaded down from the greatest to the least person in the church, the church accelerates in terms of growth and maturity. There is need for leaders and ministers to commit sound teachings and trainings to their followers.

Titus 2:1 - *"But speak thou the things which become sound doctrine."*

There is also a call for leaders in churches to invest in high quality and sound teachings of God's principles and word. It is not any kind of teaching that will mature the church, but that which is classified as 'sound' as noted in the verse above. The church should never operate in a state of ignorance. When sound doctrine and quality information is given, the church becomes stronger and matures significantly.

2. The Quality of the Gifts.

The maturity of a church also depends on the quality of its gifting and its gifted people. The higher the quality of the gifts that function in a church, the more mature the church becomes. The church at Antioch became much stronger than the church in Jerusalem because it had powerful gifts that were operational within the church. It became a strong base for releasing great apostles into the ministry.

Acts 13:1 - *"Now there were in the church that was at Antioch certain prophets and teachers; as Barnabas, and Simeon that was called Niger, and Lucius of Cyrene, and Manaen, which had been brought up with Herod the tetrarch, and Saul."*

Gifted people will raise the profile and quality of the ministry in a church. That is why it is important to identify gifts and expose them so that the church flourishes and grows further. Any authentic apostolic ministry will work on

47

developing and grooming people in the area of their gifts. However, the challenge with several churches is that there is no proper way of grooming and exposing different gifts. As a result the church remains immature.

Any church that centers all its programs and services on one powerful man or leader is in danger of not developing and maturing. Apparently it appears that there are some ministers who love to be heroes and superstars and hence they never bother to develop or train anyone in their ministries. Some easily get intimidated by those who have strong gifts and they end up spending their energy on thwarting and preventing such people from rising up in ministry. Such a stance will only limit the potential of the church to grow.

On the other hand, there are some members of the church who may also feel highly gifted and thus make the mistake of trying to outdo their leaders in proving a point that they are also gifted or better. Unfortunately such individuals never go far because if people do not learn to submit and work under authority, they can never be able to handle authority well. Anyone who despises God given leadership and authority will be despised also when he or she eventually rises up as a leader. Despising and undermining leadership is a bad seed that will manifest in those that sow such seeds.

Galatians 6:7 - *"Be not deceived; God is not mocked: for whatsoever a man soweth, that shall he also reap."*

Any church therefore that desires to be a strong apostolic ministry should deliberately expose and groom members that are gifted so that they can be able to function liberally. Gifted people should also learn to align with the apostolic vision that they serve under so as to fully add value to the ministries they belong to. This way the church will be able to rise to great levels of maturity.

3. The Quality of the Leadership

The quality of leadership also affects the stability and the maturity of the church. The leadership capacity and the quality of the leaders of the church directly reflect in the members of the church. This ultimately affects the maturity level of the church.

Ecclesiastes 10:16 - *"Woe to thee, O land, when thy king is a child, and thy princes eat in the morning!"*

The Scripture above indicates that childish and immature leadership has a negative impact on the whole church. The phrase 'when thy king is a child' implies immaturity of leadership. There are some leaders who find themselves in holding high positions but are literally clueless on how to lead. This is because such leaders still need to mature. The church can easily hit a ceiling if leaders do not develop their leadership capacity and capability to higher levels. The more stable and steadfast the leaders are, the greater the strength and maturity of the church.

It is essential for leaders to be strong and work diligently in God's house so as to propel the church higher. Leadership skills are therefore important to ensure good quality of leadership. There is also a great need for continuous improvement and up-skilling among church leaders. The only way of avoiding getting stagnant is by continuous personal development on the part of leaders. Unfortunately there are some leaders who do not see the need for improvement and there are ultimately affected by burn-out and frustration. Any great leader is ever learning and ever growing.

Apostolic Mindsets & Paradigms

Chapter Three: The Seven Levels of Maturity

2 Corinthians 3:18 - *"But we all, with open face beholding as in a glass the glory of the Lord, are changed into the same image from glory to glory, even as by the Spirit of the Lord."*

Psalms 84:7 - *"They go from strength to strength, every one of them in Zion appeareth before God."*

Defining Maturity Levels

Maturity Levels refer to the different stages that an organisation or a church goes through as it matures.

The Scripture above **(2 Corinthians 3:18)** refers to this process as moving from 'glory to glory'. It is the desire of God that His work continues to navigate from lower levels of glory to higher levels of glory. The Psalmist in Psalm

84:7 describes this as moving from **'strength to strength.'**

Psalms 84:7 - *"They go from strength to strength, every one of them in Zion appeareth before God."*

Zion refers to the church of the Living God or the Body of Christ. The church should always be moving from strength to strength. There is need for the church to continue improving the way it handles church affairs, services, planning, meetings and administration. There are certain key pillars that drive the smooth running of the church that need to evolve through the process of time. The seven maturity levels below bring out a sense of how a church evolves overtime from the starting up of a new work to the time that it grows into an apostolic and global force. Most church leaders and churches will go through these levels in some way.

The Seven Levels of Maturity

1. Opportunistic Level - "The Day of Small Things"

This is the first level of maturity in a church. The church at this stage is either still very small or is starting. At this level, there is a general level of unawareness of how to build the church. Most of the church programs are executed by trial and error with the hope that things will get better. There is also a high degree of uncertainty and fear as the church members try to understand the direction and vision of the church. There are some people who are always suspicious of new things and these will never be part of anything that is still small and starting.

This is what the Bible calls 'the day of small beginnings'. Every great vision starts small but it is important to be resolute and remain focused at this level. Some people are not willing to start small. They always want to start very high and find themselves on top. Ministry work is very hard work and therefore it requires those that are willing to work from the bottom. Anyone who is faithful in small things will be entrusted with greater things.

Zechariah 4:10 - *"For who hath despised the day of small things? for they shall rejoice, and shall see the plummet in the hand of Zerubbabel with those seven; they are the eyes of the LORD, which run to and fro through the whole earth."*

Job 8:7 - *"Though thy beginning was small, yet thy latter end should greatly increase."*

At this level, usually there are no structures that exist within the church e.g. leadership structures, financial systems or proper church administration etc. The bulk of the church members have very limited understanding of the church vision, standards and expectations. At this level, the impact of the church is still very low, but the potential is the greatest. It would be unwise for any leader at this level to compare and try to compete with churches that are well established and those that have been around for long. Faithfulness to the vision and call is the main thing that will make a difference at this stage.

2. Exploratory Maturity Level - "Study to show yourself approved"

This is a level where the church begins to gather and explore information on how to build effectively. The church also begins to explore avenues of growth and maturity. At this stage, most of the church's knowledge is theoretical and is not balanced with any experience. A lot of time is spent on researching and finding out how to do certain things e.g. how to host a conference, how to handle finances or how to setup new departments. This is an important stage because it formulates the foundation or premise upon which the church is built. Study and research at this level is absolutely critical in ensuring that the church matures.

2 Timothy 2:15 - *"Study to shew thyself approved unto God, a workman that needeth not to be ashamed, rightly dividing the word of truth."*

Getting wrong information and building on wrong fundamentals at this stage may result in a skewed foundation, which may be difficult to change at a later stage. There are some people who make assumptions at this level that will harm the church in the long run. If a minister sets a wrong precedence on handling certain ministerial issues, it will be difficult to adjust that mistake later. There are some ministers who do not bother to setup proper financial records and this becomes a wrong pattern that some struggle to adjust from.

The church at this level should begin to formulate standards and a clear way of executing ministry programs. These standards should be clearly documented and understood by members of the church.

3. Amateur Maturity Level

This is a level where some knowledge of ministry has been gained and there is a great desire to implement it. At this level, most of the ministry's programs and events are still very much sub-standard. There is a high degree of inexperience in dealing with issues that may confront the church e.g. disciplinary cases. At this level, a lot of consultation with more mature churches and ministers is required to avoid making mistakes.

At this stage, the skills level of the leadership is still low due to incompetence in dealing with new issues that arise within the church. The bulk of the church members have not been exposed and trained in various areas of ministry. At this stage again, the church begins to gain confidence because of a clear sense of direction and visible manifestations of life within the church.

One of the realities of ministry is that there are things that can only be learnt through years of ministerial experience. No matter how much one may desire to exhibit certain fruits in ministry, there are some fruits that will never manifest until one has gone through certain experiences. It is in the process of time through hard work and diligence in ministry that one begins to exhibit maturity that brings great impact.

At the amateur level, the most important thing is to follow the footsteps of those who have labored in God's vineyard longer. It is totally important to study and imitate the lifestyles of those that have succeeded in their walk. It is not necessary to reinvent the wheel if there are people to learn from.

Hebrews 6:12 - *"That ye be not slothful, but followers of them who through faith and patience inherit the promises."*

Hebrews 13:7 - *"Remember them which have the rule over you, who have spoken unto you the word of God: whose faith follow, considering the end of their conversation."*

The ability to follow the faith and conduct of those that have success stories will guarantee that the ministry will go to the next level. Some churches are always going round and round in circles and never graduate from this immature level because they do not bother to take a cue from successful ministries. I have visited some churches which continue to perennially struggle with issues that can easily be addressed through basic learning or training.

Some churches continue to struggle with simple issues like keeping time, hosting a conference and proper church service coordination. Everything that they do appears to be sub-standard to the onlooker or the person who comes into their vicinity.

The problem of remaining at the immature level for a long time is that it may result in the loss of some church members. There are certain people who get fed up if they notice that their church is not progressing to higher levels or improving its standards. On the same note there are some people who will never join a church if they feel the church is lacking certain standards that match their expectations. Every church should therefore desire to improve all the aspects of ministry and excel in all issues.

4. Repeatability Level – "The Power of Discipline and Consistency"

This is a stage where the ministry or the church begins to develop proper systems, conventional templates and structures that can be used repeatedly in performing certain tasks. This is also the level of ministry where a church begins to develop spiritual muscle through experience. The experiences of ministry at this level are crucial because they provide key learning curves for the future. The key to success at this level is consistency in ministry. The disciplines of having consistent weekly services, proper reporting lines and structures, record keeping, financial accounting and leadership meetings are examples of how to succeed at this level.

Some ministries fail to grow and mature because they lack discipline and consistency in vital things. If a leader or a ministry does not learn the importance of consistently repeating patterns overtime then they are going nowhere. There are some ministries which do not have a set pattern that they follow in running ministry programs. This creates confusion in the system because everything is haphazard. There comes a time in ministry where consistency or the lack thereof can either make or break a ministry. There are some who give up too quickly on crucial ministry activities such as weekly prayers, evangelism outreaches and the giving of tithes especially if they do not see immediate results or fruits from such activities.

There is need for ministers and ministries to remain steadfast and committed biblical and spiritual disciplines if they are to ultimately see results. It is important to note that everything gets smoother and smoother when it is repeated consistently overtime.

Galatians 6:9 - *"And let us not be weary in well doing: for in due season we shall reap, if we faint not..."*

There are some things that ministers do that will only yield results at a later season. Paul explains the importance of keeping doing good works being that they will eventually bring a good harvest. If a church is involved in regular evangelism and outreach programs, it should maintain the good work because there comes a time when the harvest of souls will be evident.

A church that hosts consistent annual conferences without fail is most likely going to become better and better in conference planning and hosting than a church which is inconsistent in conference hosting. The beauty about this level is that there is continuous improvement that comes with time because of the experience that is gained and the lessons drawn. New ideas also come through repeating certain disciplines and hence the ministry becomes more and more solid.

At this stage the church becomes more conscious of the standards and expectations required for all its programs. As a result, the church begins to follow general guidelines in planning, organisation and execution of its programs. The repeatability level is crucial because it stabilizes the church. When certain things are repeated over an extended period of time the church matures in its planning and organisation.

5. Proficiency Maturity Level (Expertise Level)

This is the level where the church experiences high levels of stability and a great level of proficiency and expertise in ministry is clearly demonstrated. At this stage, there is a clear understanding of the vision and direction of the church.

Usually at this level, the leaders in the church are skilled in divine things by reason of exposure and experience. In the book of Hebrews, the Bible talks of those who are qualified to partake of strong meat. The reason why they are qualified is because their senses are exercised in divine things through the practice.

Hebrews 5:14 - *"But strong meat belongeth to them that are of full age, even those who by reason of use have their senses exercised to discern both good and evil."*

Generally at this level, most of the church members are quite mature and can handle huge responsibilities. Most leaders and members are also able to work under pressure. Most of the church members begin to sacrifice their energy and resources into the vision because of the confidence they have in the church as well as the clear understanding of the vision.

The church also begins to experience high levels of excellence at this stage. This is because the commitment levels within the church also increase as most departments within the church begin to excel. At this level, the leaders within the church have gained experience in leading and dealing with ministerial challenges. It is the desire of every leader to get to this level where the members of the church are sold out to the vision.

Every vision requires people of great skill at some stage. These are people who can handle areas of ministry that require skilled manpower. Leaders therefore need to invest in up-skilling their churches with important abilities such as financial, technological and technical expertise. Some of the men that joined David in the wilderness were highly skilled and talented. They gave themselves to the vision and David needed such people for his success.

1 Chronicles 12:8 - *"And of the Gadites there separated themselves unto David into the hold to the wilderness men of might, and men of war fit for the battle, that could handle shield and buckler, whose faces were like the faces of lions, and were as swift as the roes upon the mountain."*

The Bible clearly states that these men were fit for the battle, they were as swift as roes on the mountains and they could handle shield and spear. This implies that these men were well trained and well groomed. Churches need such skilled people if the vision is to go any further. At this level, the church is able to handle strong teachings, corrections, and rebukes with great maturity. People are generally not offended when they are corrected or rebuked because of the maturity. There is a great sense of focus such that people are no longer spending their energies on petty and minor issues. They are driven with a sense of purpose and a desire to achieve.

6. Apostolic Maturity Level (Strategic Level)

This is a level where the church becomes apostolic in all its functions. The church begins to manifest a dominant anointing that makes it recognizable within a city or within its domain of operation. The church begins to impact the society and its surroundings in a significant way. Ministry is no longer just about the people inside the church, but there is a dimension that touches the outside world. There are people who automatically join the church at this level because of the strong apostolic anointing.

At this level, there are many gifted people that have been raised within the church. These individuals carry a strong apostolic spirit that causes them to have a great impact as they minister. The church also begins to give birth to other churches and apostolic works. Multiple churches are planted in several places across different regions. As a result, the ministry also begins to release those that are fully developed to start other apostolic works as well.

Acts 13:1-3 - *"Now there were in the church that was at Antioch certain prophets and teachers; as Barnabas, and Simeon that was called Niger, and Lucius of Cyrene, and Manaen, which had been brought up with Herod the tetrarch, and Saul. As they ministered to the Lord, and fasted, the Holy Ghost said, Separate me Barnabas and Saul for the work whereunto I have called them. And when they had fasted* *and prayed, and laid their hands on them, they sent them away."*

The church at Antioch was highly apostolic. It had many gifted people and several ministry gifts (teachers and prophets). In the Scripture above, the church released two great apostolic giants, Paul and Barnabas. This is a mark of a church that has attained apostolic maturity.

At the apostolic maturity level, the church can easily grow into a mega church. Numbers are continuously added to the church because of its influence in a territory. There are many visitors and new people who come on a weekly basis. The favour to attract people rests upon every church that has attained apostolic maturity.

Acts 2:47 - *"Praising God, and having favour with all the people. And the Lord added to the church daily such as should be saved."*

Acts 5:14 - *"And believers were the more added to the Lord, multitudes both of men and women."*

The church also begins to attract financial resources because of its impact within a region. The giving levels are generally high at this stage. There are some from outside the ministry who get compelled to sow financial seeds into the ministry. The ministry begins to be a blessing to many people including the under privileged.

Acts 4:34-35 - *"Neither was there any among them that lacked: for as many as were possessors of lands or houses sold them, and brought the prices of the things that were sold, And laid them down at the apostles' feet: and distribution was made unto every man according as he had need."*

Great doors of ministry also begin to open for the church in various forums and platforms.

Ministers and leaders become a great blessing to the Body of Christ.

1 Corinthians 16:9 - *"For a great door and effectual is opened unto me..."*

Because of the many doors that are opened at this level, the church can effectively reach out to the community. There are many kinds of community programs that can be embarked on in different sectors of society such as education, social welfare and health. Some churches may also open schools, health facilities and orphanages at this level. The apostolic maturity level is a stage that should be desired by all ministers. It literally changes the levels of ministry and the church becomes truly relevant to the community.

The level of strategic planning within the church becomes advanced as the church can project many years into the future. There is a clear strategy in terms of moving the church forward and progressing to the next level.

7. Global Maturity Level (International Level)
This is the level where the church begins to have a global impact. It is a higher level of apostolic maturity. The church, at this level is recognized globally because of its influence. At this level, the church's systems and standards begin to match global trends.

The anointing within the church at this level becomes very strong as it impacts people worldwide. The leaders within the church begin to have a global view of ministry and are often invited to speak or minister in large platforms across the world.

The church also begins to produce several products like books, magazines and DVDs that are on demand in a global scale. Such resources and products are crucial at this stage to reach out to the world. These products are life changing as there are many people that begin to fashion their lives and ministries through such resources.

Visitors from across the world also begin to visit the church on several occasions. There are people from different continents that travel to see the great work of God. The Kingdom that Solomon built attracted all kinds of people globally.

1 Kings 10:1-5 - *"And when the queen of Sheba heard of the fame of Solomon concerning the name of the LORD, she came to prove him with hard questions. And she came to Jerusalem with a very great train, with camels that bare spices, and very much gold, and precious stones: and when she was come to Solomon, she communed with him of all that was in her heart. And Solomon told her all her questions: there was not anything hid from the king, which he told her not. And when the queen of Sheba had seen all Solomon's wisdom, and the house that he had built, And the meat of his table, and the* *sitting of his servants, and the attendance of his ministers, and their apparel, and his cupbearers, and his ascent by which he went up unto the house of the LORD; there was no more spirit in her."*

This is the highest level of apostolic maturity as the church stands as a beacon of hope for the nations of the world. God is lifting up the church to such a place where it will stand out in the last days. This was echoed by the Prophet Micah where he mentions that the church will be exalted in the last days.

Micah 4:1-2 - *"But in the last days it shall come to pass, that the mountain of the house of the LORD shall be established in the top of the mountains, and it shall be exalted above the hills; and people shall flow unto it. And many nations shall come, and say, Come, and let us go up to the mountain of the LORD, and to the house of the God of Jacob; and he will teach us of his ways, and we will walk in his paths: for* *the law shall go forth of Zion, and the word of the LORD from Jerusalem.*"

God is calling ministers to raise their bar and standards in ministry and prepare for global impact. The church will be the only hope for the social and economic challenges of the nations. There will be many that will flock to the church for answers and solutions.

The Impact of Maturity Levels in a Church

1. It affects reception levels

The level of maturity of a church affects the reception levels of the church e.g. how people receive the word and handle ministry in general. If the church is still immature, it cannot receive higher dimensions of ministry because of a lack of readiness to digest higher things.

Hebrews 5:12 - *"For when for the time ye ought to be teachers, ye have need that one teach you again which be the first principles of the oracles of God; and are become such as have need of milk, and not of strong meat."*

There are things that can be taught in one church and not be taught in another because of maturity levels. I remember teaching the word of God in a certain church on the baptism of the Holy Spirit some years ago. I ministered that word but I could tell that the people were not ready to receive such a word. This was primarily because the church had not previously been exposed to such teachings. I ended up praying for only two people out of a congregation of about 60 people to receive the baptism of the Holy Spirit with the evidence of speaking in tongues.

Ministers should work diligently to ensure that churches mature and that the people move from one level of maturity to another. The church should therefore be exposed to the full counsel of the Word of God.

2. It affects capacity levels

The capacity of a church also depends on the maturity of the church. Capacity refers to the ability to grasp, comprehend and handle ministerial work and challenges. An immature church cannot handle multiple responsibilities because of the strains that responsibility brings.

Hebrews 5:12 - *"For when for the time ye ought to be teachers, ye have need that one teach you again which be the first principles of the oracles of God; and are become such as have need of milk, and not of strong meat."*

The saints in the Scripture above were supposed to be at the level of teachers but they were still in need of teaching because of low capacity levels. It is the responsibility of leaders to ensure that the church develops its capacity overtime. If the church fails to develop its capacity, then it is not maturing and not getting any better. This then results in some church members complaining when they are assigned responsibilities by their leaders. Generally, I have discovered that complaining about crucial ministerial work and activities is a sign of immaturity. Some who are extremely immature literally begin to dodge church meetings and services. However when the church matures, the key people will have great capacity to handle responsibility.

3. It affects giving levels

The giving levels of a church are related to the maturity levels of the church as well. How much people give is influenced by the maturity of the church. Generally people tend to give more to well established and more mature churches than to struggling and limping churches. This is because people tend to trust churches with more established systems and structures than those who do not have.

Ministers should therefore work on propelling their ministries to higher levels of maturity so that the church becomes more solid and established. The grace of giving increases as the church matures. The churches of Macedonia excelled very well in the grace of giving.

2 Corinthians 8:1-6 - *"Moreover, brethren, we do you to wit of the grace of God bestowed on the churches of Macedonia; For to their power, I bear record, yea, and beyond their power they were willing of themselves; Praying us with much intreaty that we would receive the gift, and take upon us the fellowship of the ministering to the saints. And this they did, not as we hoped, but first gave their own selves to the Lord, and unto us by the will of God. Insomuch that we desired Titus, that as he had begun, so he would also finish in you the same grace also."*

2 Corinthians 8:7 - *"Therefore, as ye abound in everything, in faith, and utterance, and*

81

knowledge, and in all diligence, and in your love to us, see that ye abound in this grace also."

The Macedonian churches abounded in this grace of giving which the church at Corinth had not developed. If any leader desires to see an increase in the grace of giving, he or she should work on maturing the believers and raising the profile of the church.

4. It affects interpretation levels

The maturity level of the church also affects the way the church interprets certain things. Some things may be perceived as tough if the maturity levels are still low. A general basic doctrinal word that is ministered in one church may be interpreted as a very hard word.

Hebrews 5:12 - *"For when for the time ye ought to be teachers, ye have need that one teach you again which be the first principles of the oracles of God; and are become such as have need of milk, and not of strong meat."*

82

Hebrews 5:14 - *"But strong meat belongeth to them that are of full age, even those who by reason of use have their senses exercised to discern both good and evil."*

We are living in times where the word of God has been compromised in some circles. People are not taught the full counsel of the word and sin issues are never addressed. Therefore, the lifestyles of people are not changing at all. Ministers should be careful to avoid compromise because it causes the church to limp and remain immature. The declaration of sound doctrine and the full counsel of the word of God must never cease.

Titus 1:9 - *"Holding fast the faithful word as he hath been taught, that he may be able by sound doctrine both to exhort and to convince the gainsayers."*

Titus 2:1 - *"But speak thou the things which become sound doctrine."*

It is only when the church matures, that people begin to interpret things correctly and accurately.

5. It affects discernment levels

There is a general lack of discernment in the church if the maturity levels are low. The carnality that existed in the church of Corinth caused them not to discern well resulting in them failing to deal with disciplinary issues.

1 Corinthains 3:1-3 - *"And I, brethren, could not speak unto you as unto spiritual, but as unto carnal, even as unto babes in Christ. I have fed you with milk, and not with meat: for hitherto ye were not able to bear it, neither yet now are ye able. For ye are yet carnal: for whereas there is among you envying, and strife, and divisions, are ye not carnal, and walk as men?"*

1 Corinthians 5:3 - *"For I verily, as absent in body, but present in spirit, have judged already, as though I were present, concerning him that hath so done this deed."*

Discernment refers to spiritual sensitivity and the ability to pass accurate judgment over issues. Discernment only grows and comes when the church matures. The ability to separate and judge what is right and what is wrong comes with maturity. Being able to separate error from the truth increases as the church matures. Distinguishing between good and evil is for those who have increased in maturity.

Hebrews 5:14 - *"But strong meat belongeth to them that are of full age, even those who by reason of use have their senses exercised to discern both good and evil."*

There are some Christians who cannot identify deception or error. They fall into all sorts of traps of the enemy because of lack of maturity. They easily embrace anything that looks like church but they cannot see the spirit behind some things. It is important for Pastors and ministers to safeguard their flock by ensuring that they are stirred up towards maturity.

Tools for Developing Maturity Levels

Whilst it takes time to develop maturity levels in a church, there are some key things that help to propel a church higher.

1. Training of People

Nothing equips the church better than the training of people. Training equips the saints with the necessary tools for the ministry. Many churches and people are starved of training. All they get are motivational speeches which are good but not effective in imparting practical ministry knowledge. It is not enough to preach exciting messages but it is absolutely crucial to train people on practical ways of dealing with life issues.

There is need for balance in training. Practical issues such as relationships, marriage, financial management and time management should be balanced with issues of spiritual disciplines like prayer, fasting, giving and the study of the Word. The ultimate desire of every leader is to produce a balanced church which is relevant in the diverse issues of life.

It is very common to find churches are really not balanced in their approach. At times highly spiritual people are found messing up in their churches particularly on simple practical day to day life issues. On the other hand, there are those who take the other extreme of concentrating on life skills issues only whilst neglecting some key spiritual disciplines. This creates a serious imbalance in the church and the church hardly matures in the long run.

Any serious leader will develop a training program to mature the church. There are many different platforms of training that can be employed such as Bible School, Seminars, Short Courses and Retreats. Proper deliberate efforts to train and equip people will go a long way in maturing and developing the church. Jesus taught his disciples to pray. John the Baptist taught his disciples to pray.

Luke 11:1 - *"And it came to pass, that, as he was praying in a certain place, when he ceased, one of his disciples said unto him, Lord, teach us to pray, as John also taught his disciples."*

In the Old Testament, there where schools of prophets, in these, prophetic sons were rose. All these were training grounds for equipping generations. When people are well trained, they serve God effectively. Lack of ministerial acumen is a direct result of lack of proper training. Training matures the church to healthy levels. Once the church matures it attains new levels of grace and anointing.

2. Teaching of the Word

The Word grounds people to become solid Christians. The teaching of the Word should be done on all platforms possible in all types of meetings. People should never cease to be taught the Word of God.

Deuteronomy 6:6-9 - *"And these words, which I command thee this day, shall be in thine heart: And thou shalt teach them diligently unto thy children, and shalt talk of them when thou sittest in thine house, and when thou walkest by the way, and when thou liest down, and when thou risest up. And thou shalt bind them for a sign upon thine hand, and they shall be as frontlets between thine eyes. And thou shalt write them upon the posts of thy house, and on thy gates."*

In the Old Testament, great emphasis was placed on the need to teach the Word of God continuously. It is important to have such an attitude because it is one of the ways of fostering growth and maturity. Teaching of the Word implies imparting sound doctrine in the lives of the people. The church should be well taught in terms of biblical and doctrinal doctrines. Unfortunately there is a general lack of doctrinal knowledge in many churches. These are called the fundamental doctrines of Christ according to the book of Hebrews.

Hebrews 6:1-2 - *"Therefore leaving the principles of the doctrine of Christ, let us go on unto perfection; not laying again the foundation of repentance from dead works, and of faith toward God, Of the doctrine of baptisms, and of laying on of hands, and of resurrection of the dead, and of eternal judgment."*

Churches need to mature in teaching and handling sound doctrine. The Bible warns of the departure from sound doctrine that will take place in the last days. When the church departs from sound doctrine, it becomes vulnerable to deceptive spirits.

1 Timothy 4:1 - *"Now the Spirit speaketh expressly, that in the latter times some shall depart from the faith, giving heed to seducing spirits, and doctrines of devils..."*

2 Timothy 4:3-4 - *"For the time will come when they will not endure sound doctrine; but after their own lusts shall they heap to themselves teachers, having itching ears; And they shall turn away their ears from the truth, and shall be turned unto fables."*

It is the teaching ministry that will safeguard the church from false teachings and false teachers. When the Word of God is well taught, it anchors the church. A church with a strong teaching ministry is not easily shaken by various winds of doctrines.

3. Raising of Leaders

The more the leaders are raised, the more stable the church becomes. As the church seeks to grow and mature, there has to be a lot of work in grooming and raising leaders. New leaders increase the levels of anointing in a church. This is because they bring diverse skills and gifts to leadership.

There are different kinds of leaders that can be raised depending on the size and complexity of the church. These leaders range from those that serve in different portfolios, departmental leaders (deacons), elders, ministers, associate pastors, pastors and evangelists to mention a few.

A church that desires to grow in the apostolic should develop a system that raises and releases leaders. There should always be room for the growth and development of leaders in a church. Leadership trainings and seminars for different types of leaders are crucial for this process of leadership development to take place.

At several stages in the lifespan of the church, there are people who mature and become ready for leadership. It is important to identify and work with such individuals. Ignoring potential leaders may create unnecessary tension and strains in church because people are misplaced. When gifted people and potential leaders are misplaced, the church can easily become ineffective.

4. Solid Structures

The setting up of solid church structures is essential for maturing the church. A church that operates without proper structures will hit a ceiling and will not mature beyond a certain level. Whilst the anointing draws people to the house of God, it is the solidness of church structures that support and sustain the ministry overtime.

93

Structures that need to be taken note of in a church or a ministry include good leadership structures, clear reporting lines, accountability structures, cell group structures, the order of church services, financial systems and employment policies. Many people ignore the importance of such structures yet these are the things that can make or break a church. Churches nowadays are under great scrutiny from government officials, and it is completely necessary to have clean and clear structures in a church.

Some ministers have been found wanting and caught up in financial scandals because of weak financial systems. Other churches have lost membership because of abuses that are caused by poor church structures. As the ministry grows, it employs many people into the church office. Organograms, salary structures and employment policies need to be fully implemented. Quite often churches have mediocre standards when it comes to human resources and employment policies. It is dangerous to have church workers who do not have employment contracts and have no clue of how much they earn. Some do not even have office space to work from and end up just idling in the ministry. There was a church that I used to pass through on one of the streets in my city on my way to work. I would always get amazed to see several church employees spending their entire day basking in the sun instead of working. Such things should be avoided at all costs.

There is a stage in ministry that requires diligent and good management. When God entrusts a church with resources and people, He expects those that have been appointed as stewards over that inheritance to do their part in ensuring that all things given are well managed and accounted for.

1 Corinthians 4:2 - *"Moreover it is required in stewards, that a man be found faithful."*

Matthew 25:23 - *"His lord said unto him, Well done, good and faithful servant; thou hast been faithful over a few things, I will make thee ruler over many things: enter thou into the joy of thy lord."*

Many ministers see the importance of believing God for resources. But when resources have come, what is needed is good management not faith. Good management and administration will be evident in the kinds of systems and structures that the church sets up. The church in the 21st century needs to work diligently in the implementation of solid structures and systems.

5. Exposure

One of the other greatest keys to maturity is exposure. The word exposure means 'the act of subjecting someone to an influencing experience'. When ministers, ministries and churches are exposed, they can easily increase in maturity levels. There are certain life experiences that provoke and challenge people to desire to go higher.

The challenge facing ministers and churches is a lack of exposure. There is a great desire in many people to do great exploits for God, but they operate in a little closed-up corner and have no idea what is happening elsewhere. I have often talked to people who have expressed that they believe God will take them to the nations of the world but they are not doing anything to get themselves exposed to the levels that they believe they are going. When the children of Israel where about to enter the land of Canaan, spies were sent to view the land and have a feel of how the land appeared.

Numbers 13:17-25 - *"And Moses sent them to spy out the land of Canaan, and said unto them, Get you up this way southward, and go up into the mountain: And see the land, what it is; and the people that dwelleth therein, whether they be strong or weak, few or many; And what the* *land is that they dwell in, whether it be good or bad; and what cities they be that they dwell in, whether in tents, or in strong holds; And what the land is, whether it be fat or lean, whether there be wood therein, or not. And be ye of good courage, and bring of the fruit of the land. Now the time was the time of the first ripe grapes."*

Numbers 13:25 - *"And they returned from searching of the land after forty days."*

Any church that desires to mature into the apostolic should be well informed and well exposed. There can never be any change of maturity level until perceptions change. Exposure comes through many platforms. It may come through travelling and visiting places. It may also come through study and research. Sometimes it is crucial to visit those that have achieved greater things to get important insights of how to achieve greatness.

There are some ministers who are so proud such that they will never dare learn from anyone. Over the years, I have encountered leaders who never acknowledge the success of other churches. They continue suffering on issues that could be avoided by simply engaging those that are a step ahead. Unfortunately in the apostolic, consultation, learning and acquisition of wisdom cannot be avoided. This is the only way that guarantees that the church will not hit a ceiling. Apostolic people are well connected and are always getting new ideas on how to go higher.

Once a church is exposed to greater levels of ministry, leadership and excellence it will find new vigor and strength to go higher. It is important for leaders not to allow their churches to be confined in a little corner such that there is no room to maneuver. God desires better things for ministers, leaders and churches.

Apostolic Mindsets & Paradigms

Chapter Four: Apostolic Mindsets

Apostolic Mindsets

In order for the church to progress swiftly and come into full alignment with the will and purposes of God, there is need for leaders to move to an **"Apostolic Leadership"** mindset and paradigm. This does not imply that Pastors, Ministers and Leaders should be called "Apostles", but it refers to the development and implementation of an Apostolic Leadership style which will facilitate the rapid acceleration and growth of churches.

The role of the Apostolic Leadership is by its very nature visionary whereas the role of an ordinary Pastor is more of shepherding the flock. Part of the process of transitioning to the apostolic model of leadership involves a mindset change.

Proverbs 23:7 - *"For as he thinketh in his heart, so is he: Eat and drink, saith he to thee; but his heart is not with thee."*

Unless one shifts their kind of thinking to the apostolic framework, there can never be a change in the leadership style. The health and progress of any church or organisation is directly affected by the mindsets of its leadership.

Defining Mindsets

A mindset is an established set of attitudes that are held by someone. A mindset can also be defined as a fixed mental attitude or disposition that predetermines a person's responses to and interpretations of situations.

Mindsets are therefore ideas and attitudes that affect how a person approaches a situation. The way a person approaches the work of ministry is a result of the mindset that he or she holds.

Characteristics of Mindsets

1. **Mindsets are mental attitudes** that have been formed over the years. Normally it takes a long time for mindsets to be formed in people or organisations.

2. **Mindsets are concepts**, beliefs, doctrines, ideologies, principles, traditions, habits and character that one has lived with all his life. When mindsets have been formed they affect the belief systems and ideologies that a person lives with. This is also true of organisations and churches.

3. **Mindsets are strong and deep-rooted convictions** in the mind and heart of a person, and may not necessarily be correct. Mindsets are so powerful and yet sometimes particular mindsets may be out of line with the will of God.

4. **Mindsets are personal opinions** that one has lived with and are not willing to give up. Normally it is very difficult to throw away a mindset that has formed part of a person's lifestyle over a long period of time.

5. **Mindsets are also thinking patterns** or perspectives to life that are not easy to depart from, even when the person is willing or wants to change.

From the above characteristics, it is easy to note that mindsets have a great effect and influence on people and organisations. Pastors and leaders should therefore work on ensuring that they cultivate the right kind of mindsets that align with divine purpose and will. If this does not happen, the church will never reach and attain its maximum potential.

Romans 12:2 - *"And be not conformed to this world: but be ye transformed by the renewing of* *your mind, that ye may prove what is that good, and acceptable, and perfect, will of God."*

Renewal of the mind is an essential process that fosters growth and maturity in the church. It takes a lot of discipline to renew the mind. Study, research, learning and exposure are some of the ways to renew the mind.

Leaders and Pastors need to be studious in order to renew their mind. It is important to get the right kind of literature that fosters the renewal of the mind. Reading and studying the Bible, Christian literature, leadership material and biographies helps this process. It is also necessary to seek counsel and wisdom from the right kind of people as well as to visit the right kind of places.

Three things affected by mindsets in a Church or a Ministry

1. The Health of the church.

The health of a church refers to the well-being, strength and fitness of a church. When one walks into a church it is fairly simple to tell from the atmosphere whether it is healthy or not. Apparently it is easy to gauge the health of a church by the vibrancy that prevails in the atmosphere. There are certain places where there is no life. The people struggle to pray, to worship, to praise when everything in the church is very dull and gloomy.

How healthy a church becomes is directly influenced by the mindsets of its leaders. These mindsets are imparted into the congregants and the church at large. The mindsets of the leaders ultimately form the dominant mindset that prevails in the church. A church can become unhealthy if the mindsets of the leaders are not aligned properly to God and His Word. Some churches get into stagnation because leaders cannot think beyond the level where they have reached. Stagnation usually causes inactivity, sluggishness and inefficiency in the church.

A healthy church on the other hand is a church that is well balanced and produces healthy people who are well taught and groomed in divine things. To maintain a healthy church, it takes a lot of effort to invest in the right kind of mindset. Usually in a healthy church, there is a strong manifestation of the Presence of God, there is great joy among the people and the people express passion for what they do. The desire of every Pastor should be to maintain a good state of health in the church.

2. The Progress of the Church.
The progress of the church is a consequence of the mental capacity and mindsets of its leaders.

Leaders who have 'small' minds will limit how far a church can go. There are leaders who easily get satisfied with mediocre standards. As a result they stop dreaming and projecting into the future.

The church ultimately remains at the same level or dwindles overtime. Anytime a church stops progressing, there are bound to be challenges that begin to hit the church. One of the challenges is that people generally become religious instead of worshipping God in spirit and in truth. Some begin to gossip and spend time on things that do not progress the church forward.

Many people generally get frustrated if an unprogressive and stagnant environment prevails in a church. These will ultimately leave the church because they feel the church has no room to grow any further. They will look for places or churches which are more progressive.

On the other hand, if leaders continue to advance their mindsets, this will also cause the church to respond accordingly. The church is bound to move with speed if the leaders are always aiming for higher levels of ministry. The speed at which the church moves and progresses is directly influenced by the prevailing mindsets.

3. The Capacity of the Church.

The capacity, ability and capability of the church are a product of mindsets that are at work in that church. There are some people that will not stay in a church because of limitations that prevail in their leaders' minds. There are some resources that God will not entrust to some leaders because of their way of thinking.

Five Types of Leadership Mindsets

1. Juvenile Mindset

A juvenile mindset is an attention seeking, self-seeking and self-conscious mindset. This is a mindset which is self-conscious and self-seeking when it comes to ministerial issues. There is a high level of self-awareness and leaders are preoccupied about themselves than the work at hand. Such awareness can impair one's ability to perform complex actions or tasks. This normally happens in the early stages of ministry. Moses went through this phase in his ministry.

Exodus 3:11 - *"And Moses said unto God, Who am I, that I should go unto Pharaoh, and that I should bring forth the children of Israel out of Egypt?"*

Moses could not believe that he could carry out the task that God was assigning him. It is sad that some leaders never seem to transition from this type of mindset to a place where they allow God to fully use them.

Exodus 4:1 - *"And Moses answered and said, but, behold, they will not believe me, nor hearken unto my voice: for they will say, The LORD hath not appeared unto thee."*

Exodus 4:10 - *"And Moses said unto the LORD, O my Lord, I am not eloquent, neither heretofore, nor since thou hast spoken unto thy servant: but I am slow of speech, and of a slow tongue."*

Leaders need to quickly deal with unhealthy levels of self-consciousness because it impairs their effectiveness. There is need to put faith and confidence in God when it comes to ministry work.

Exodus 4:11–12 - *"And the LORD said unto him, Who hath made man's mouth? or who maketh the dumb, or deaf, or the seeing, or the blind? have not I the LORD? Now therefore go,* *and I will be with thy mouth, and teach thee what thou shalt say."*

In ministry it is the Lord that calls people and equips them. Pastors should therefore, always focus on the Lord for help and confidence. Paul indicates in his letter to the Corinthians that his sufficiency came from the fact that God was the one who called him. Whenever God calls a person, he also empowers and equips that person.

2 Corinthians 3:5-6 - *"Not that we are sufficient of ourselves to think anything as of ourselves; but our sufficiency is of God; Who also hath made us able ministers of the new testament; not of the letter, but of the spirit: for the letter killeth, but the spirit giveth life."*

A juvenile mindset is also one that gets bogged down with people affairs and that is primarily what people are saying. Some leaders are extremely affected by every negative comment that is passed about them or their churches. This is because their mindsets are still juvenile and such leaders need to develop their mindsets. Some literally walk into depression because of gossip. Any great leader cannot run away from negative criticism. It is the ability to handle criticism that makes great apostolic leaders. Paul exhorts Timothy to focus on ministry work like a soldier and not to be bogged down with civilian affairs.

2 Timothy 2:3-4 - *"Thou therefore endure hardness, as a good soldier of Jesus Christ. No man that wareth entangleth himself with the affairs of this life; that he may please him who hath chosen him to be a soldier."*

Ephesians 4:14 - *"That we henceforth be no more children, tossed to and fro, and carried about with every wind of doctrine, by the sleight of men, and cunning craftiness, whereby they lie in wait to deceive."*

A juvenile mindset is also an attention seeking mindset which is characterised by show off and external displays. There are some ministers who love show off and external displays. Their ministries are preoccupied by the need to please people and ensure that they get all the attention. This is the lowest level of ministry.

1 Corinthians 13:11 - *"When I was a child, I spake as a child, I understood as a child, I thought as a child: but when I became a man, I put away childish things."*

Any minister who focuses on maintaining popularity at the expense of God's Word is still a juvenile. Such ministers also focus on the benefits of ministry more that the work of ministry. It is this type of mindset that is highly dependent on what ministry gives to the minister more than what the minister gives into ministry. It is unfortunate that they are leaders who start well in ministry but eventually end up enriching themselves in dubious ways through ministry.

Colossians 4:17 - *"And say to Archippus, Take heed to the ministry which thou hast received in the Lord, that thou fulfil it."*

Leaders should not dwell on childish things that do not change anything. There should be a realization that ministry is a calling from God that should be fulfilled. Any leader who commits himself or herself fully to God's work will be blessed of the Lord in the long run.

Hebrews 6:10 - *"For God is not unrighteous to forget your work and labour of love, which ye have shewed toward his name, in that ye have ministered to the saints, and do minister."*

2. Sonship Mindset

The second type of mindset is the sonship mindset. At this level, a leader realises that they should demonstrate the maturity of

115

sonship. When a person is born again, they automatically become a child of God. But in the Kingdom of God, it is important to eventually become a mature son. This maturity into sonship is a process that comes through cultivating a relationship with God. This is the first level of developing an apostolic mindset. Anyone who wants to be apostolic should firstly work on developing a sonship mindset.

Romans 8:14 - *"For as many as are led by the Spirit of God, they are the sons of God."*

Romans 8:14 above indicates that one of the marks of true sonship is the ability to be led by the Spirit of God. This means that it is not enough to be a child of God, but the ability to obey God and the promptings of the Spirit will distinguish between mature and immature sons. Obedience is one of the greatest tests in the school of sonship. Sonship implies loyalty to God and to the work of ministry. Jesus as a

Son demonstrated great levels of obedience despite the sufferings that he went through.

Hebrews 5:5-9 - *"So also Christ glorified not himself to be made an high priest; but he that said unto him, Thou art my Son, today have I begotten thee. As he saith also in another place, Thou art a priest for ever after the order of Melchizedec. Who in the days of his flesh, when he had offered up prayers and supplications with strong crying and tears unto him that was able to save him from death, and was heard in that he feared; Though he were a Son, yet learned he obedience by the things which he suffered; And being made perfect, he became the author of eternal salvation unto all them that obey him."*

The mindset that has developed into son-ship is characterised by taking responsibility and being accountable. It is a mindset that takes ownership of God's work and desires to build the work.

Hebrews 3:4-6 - *"For every house is builded by some man; but he that built all things is God. And Moses verily was faithful in all his house, as a servant, for a testimony of those things which were to be spoken after; But Christ as a son over his own house; whose house are we, if we hold fast the confidence and the rejoicing of the hope firm unto the end."*

A sonship mindset is a mindset that focuses on building the work of God. There is need to develop a son-ship mindset and focus on building God's House. The work of building the Kingdom of God should never be taken for granted. Ministry is not a playground for gimmicks and promotion of personal agendas. There is need to realize that God is serious with his work and He desires those that can labour faithfully so as to fulfill His purposes.

3. Destiny Mindset

This is an apostolic mindset that is destiny oriented. It is a mindset that desires to see fulfillment of destiny. Destiny is embedded in all the children of God and it is essential to see it unfolding. There is a place that God has ordained for all those that walk with Him. It should be the passion of every leader to get to that place.

Jeremiah 1:5 - *"Before I formed thee in the belly I knew thee; and before thou camest forth out of the womb I sanctified thee, and I ordained thee a prophet unto the nations."*

It is not enough to know that one is called by God. It is important to align every faculty of one's being towards the fulfillment of that destiny. The path towards that place has many challenges, but a person with a destiny mindset keeps pushing towards the fulfillment of God's purposes.

A destiny mindset is also finishing mindset that focuses on targets and goals ahead.

Philippians 3:12 - *"Not as though I had already attained, either were already perfect: but I follow after, if that I may apprehend that for which also I am apprehended of Christ Jesus."*

Philippians 3:14 - *"I press toward the mark for the prize of the high calling of God in Christ Jesus."*

Leaders should not just focus on doing divine work and assignments but they should focus on finishing the assignments that God has given. There is need to drive towards finishing the course that God has defined. Paul came to that place in his life where he knew in himself that he had fulfilled the will of God in his generation.

2 Timothy 4:7 - *"I have fought a good fight, I have finished my course, I have kept the faith."*

This is also mindset which focuses on making an impact on the people of God. Ministry has to transform lives and take people to higher levels. It is important that all leaders should make an impact in the Kingdom of God. Lives of people should be transformed as leaders serve and minister in God's House. There is nothing as gratifying as knowing that God is using an individual to transform many lives. Ultimately, the work of every individual is evident through the kind of fruits that he or she produces.

Matthew 7:15-19 - *"Beware of false prophets, which come to you in sheep's clothing, but inwardly they are ravening wolves. Ye shall know them by their fruits. Do men gather grapes of thorns, or figs of thistles? Even so every good tree bringeth forth good fruit; but a corrupt tree bringeth forth evil fruit. A good tree cannot bring forth evil fruit, neither can a corrupt tree bring forth good fruit. Every tree that bringeth not forth* *good fruit is hewn down, and cast into the fire. Wherefore by their fruits ye shall know them.*"

The Bible in the Scripture above warns of false prophets who produce evil fruit. Fruit is evident in the character of the people who pass through the hands of a minister. If people who pass through the hands of a minister are rebellious and shrewd in their character, then there is a problem in the ministry of that leader. There are some ministers who are always producing arrogant and proud people.

It is crucial for every genuine leader to produce good fruit that will last and remain. Churches and ministries should be impact driven so as to make the difference that is needed in people's lives.

The Destiny Mindset is also a target oriented mindset. Ministers should learn to set targets for themselves and their churches. No effective leader can lead without setting targets ahead of him. It is the ability to concentrate on targets that will keep a minister in the path of destiny. Without targets there is a high propensity to go off-track. A few times I have seen leaders who seemingly do not have targets that they are working on at any given time. This often causes idleness and slothfulness in the life of a leader.

There are some Pastors who have church offices that they do not use. Church offices are just places for appointments and meetings but no real ministerial work takes place there. This is recipe for disaster and it will eventually show in the quality of the work that is produced. One does not have to announce to the whole world that they are working hard. Where there is hard work, there is evidence that is seen in the quality of the work. Hard work always reflects in excellence and distinction that is produced. I have often told some people that I can tell the difference between someone who has put effort and hard work to an assignment and one who has done a shoddy work.

There is a call from God to all leaders to start focusing on what really matters. There are targets that God is expecting His people to fulfill.

4. Strategic Mindset

A Strategic Mindset is an apostolic mindset that strategically focuses on expanding and spreading the apostolic vision. It is a mindset that focuses on spreading the work and anointing of God to many territories. Anyone who is in the apostolic ministry will have a strong inclination and desire for possessing territory. An apostolic leader will never be satisfied by being confined to one area. There is an aggressive passion in the heart of every apostolic person to possess God ordained territories. Caleb is an example of a man who had such a strategic mindset. This is echoed in his statement where he expressed his desire to possess his God given inheritance.

Joshua 14:6–13 - *"Then the children of Judah came unto Joshua in Gilgal: and Caleb the son of Jephunneh the Kenezite said unto him, Thou knowest the thing that the LORD said unto Moses the man of God concerning me and thee in Kadeshbarnea. Forty years old was I when Moses the servant of the LORD sent me from Kadeshbarnea to espy out the land; and I brought him word again as it was in mine heart. Nevertheless my brethren that went up with me made the heart of the people melt: but I wholly followed the LORD my God. And Moses sware on that day, saying, Surely the land whereon thy feet have trodden shall be thine inheritance, and thy children's forever, because thou hast wholly followed the LORD my God. And now, behold, the LORD hath kept me alive, as he said, these forty and five years, even since the LORD spake this word unto Moses, while the children of Israel wandered in the wilderness: and now, lo, I am this day fourscore and five years old. As yet I am as strong this day as I was in the day that Moses sent me: as my strength was* *then, even so is my strength now, for war, both to go out, and to come in. Now therefore give me this mountain, whereof the LORD spake in that day; for thou heardest in that day how the Anakims were there, and that the cities were great and fenced: if so be the LORD will be with me, then I shall be able to drive them out, as the LORD said. And Joshua blessed him, and gave unto Caleb the son of Jephunneh Hebron for an inheritance."*

Caleb was blessed by Joshua and he was given the inheritance he desired. The type of mindset that a leader exhibits will either cause them to inherit their possessions or not. There are some leaders who do not seem to have a big appetite for territory. This only limits their sphere of influence and how much they can possess. But apostolic people are always pushing for more as long as God is leading them.

Obadiah 1:17 - *"But upon mount Zion shall be deliverance, and there shall be holiness; and the house of Jacob shall possess their possessions."*

This type of mindset causes one to be a strategic thinker or dreamer. There is a strategic ability to penetrate into different areas and territories with a desire to influence and expand the Kingdom of God. There are many places where the Gospel still needs to be preached. Any apostolic person will long for the spread of God's Word to all the corners of the earth. There are places where the strongholds of the devil have reigned and dominated. These places can only be penetrated and infiltrated by apostolic leaders that can change the atmospheres in such places. The kingdoms of this world should become the kingdoms of our God.

Revelation 11:15 - *"And the seventh angel sounded; and there were great voices in heaven, saying, The kingdoms of this world are become*
127

the kingdoms of our Lord, and of his Christ; and he shall reign for ever and ever."

There are cities, villages, towns and nations that still need to be taken for Jesus. It requires people who are violent and aggressive to take such territory. This can only happen when the apostolic anointing rests upon the people of God.

Matthew 11:12 - *"And from the days of John the Baptist until now the kingdom of heaven suffereth violence, and the violent take it by force."*

A strategic mindset is also a generational mindset that seeks to raise and impact future generations. Apostolic people are not myopic but they think and build for generations to come. Leaders should think strategically as they consider the generations to come. In a church, a leader should identify different layers of generations that exist and come up with

128

strategies of how to groom and raise them. From the people who are most senior in the church down to the children in Sunday School, programs have to be designed that will impart generational legacy to them. The eye for growth, expansion and future is required in every serious apostolic leader.

2 Timothy 2:2 - *"And the things that thou hast heard of me among many witnesses, the same commit thou to faithful men, who shall be able to teach others also."*

There are things that need to be taught and released to younger and upcoming generations. The general trend in the church has been to ignore those that are still young and immature. This only causes chaos and complications when current leaders leave their office. There should be a system and a way of imparting divine things to those that are faithful. It is important to notice that Paul in the scripture above emphasizes the need to commit divine things to

129

faithful men. It will be a great mistake for any leader to try and commit divine secrets to those that have not proved to be faithful.

5. Kingdom Mindset

The Kingdom Mindset is an apostolic mindset that is holistic. It is a mindset that looks at the bigger picture of ministry. It is also a mindset that understands the Body of Christ and how it functions. Such a mindset desires the expansion of God's kingdom. It is not limited or confined to a local church or ministry. Jesus had such a mindset because he always taught about the kingdom of God and the kingdom of heaven.

Matthew 13:44 - *"Again, the kingdom of heaven is like unto treasure hid in a field; the which when a man hath found, he hideth, and for joy thereof goeth and selleth all that he hath, and buyeth that field."*

Matthew 13:45 - *"Again, the kingdom of heaven is like unto a merchant man, seeking goodly pearls."*

Matthew 13:47 - *"Again, the kingdom of heaven is like unto a net, that was cast into the sea, and gathered of every kind."*

Such a mindset embraces the entire kingdom view and is not just limited to earthly things but even heavenly things. People with a kingdom mindset invest not only in this life but also the life to come. The Kingdom of God is not just here on earth but it is also a heavenly kingdom that includes those in heaven.

Hebrews 12:22-24 - *"But ye are come unto mount Sion, and unto the city of the living God, the heavenly Jerusalem, and to an innumerable company of angels, To the general assembly and church of the firstborn, which are written in heaven, and to God the Judge of all, and to the spirits of just men made perfect, And to Jesus* *the mediator of the new covenant, and to the blood of sprinkling, that speaketh better things than that of Abel."*

Leaders should always look at the bigger picture as they lead so that they can effectively raise balanced people with a complete understanding of kingdom dynamics. There are some believers who have no clue about life after death, the resurrection of the dead and eternal judgment. This is a manifestation of a limited kingdom view. But there is need to run the race with full understanding and revelation.

1 Corinthians 9:24-25 - *"Know ye not that they which run in a race run all, but one receiveth the prize? So run, that ye may obtain. And every man that striveth for the mastery is temperate in all things. Now they do it to obtain a corruptible crown; but we an incorruptible."*

Colossians 3:1-4 - *"If ye then be risen with Christ, seek those things which are above,* *where Christ sitteth on the right hand of God. Set your affection on things above, not on things on the earth. For ye are dead, and your life is hid with Christ in God. When Christ, who is our life, shall appear, then shall ye also appear with him in glory."*

The kingdom mindset is also Christ like mindset that is willing to go through sacrifices and suffering for the sake of the greater kingdom. The Bible encourages that the mind of Christ should grow and develop in His people. It is a selfless mindset that is prepared to go through challenges and suffering.

Philippians 2:5-8 - *"Let this mind be in you, which was also in Christ Jesus: Who, being in the form of God, thought it not robbery to be equal with God: But made himself of no reputation, and took upon him the form of a servant, and was made in the likeness of men: And being found in fashion as a man, he* *humbled himself, and became obedient unto death, even the death of the cross."*

Apostolic people are prepared to go through tough experiences as long as they are in the will of God. Sadly a lot of leaders nowadays are not prepared to go through any kind of suffering. There is a general assumption that any kind of suffering is not permissible. It has become taboo that a minister of God's Word can go through suffering and challenges. Yet the Bible indicates that believers may go through all kinds of persecution and suffering.

Romans 8:17-18 - *"And if children, then heirs; heirs of God, and joint-heirs with Christ; if so be that we suffer with him, that we may be also glorified together. For I reckon that the sufferings of this present time are not worthy to be compared with the glory which shall be revealed in us."*

Some, because of pressure, have even succumbed to worldly standards and compromised their position as Christians. It is through avoiding challenges that many leaders have missed God. They have literally side tracked as they avoided uncomfortable and bumpy pathways. Apostolic people however rise up to higher levels of glory through challenges and suffering.

The Apostle Paul also displayed such a selfless mindset that desired to build the Kingdom of God.

Acts 20:24 - *"But none of these things move me, neither count I my life dear unto myself, so that I might finish my course with joy, and the ministry, which I have received of the Lord Jesus, to testify the gospel of the grace of God."*

2 Corinthians 11:23-28 - *"Are they ministers of Christ? (I speak as a fool) I am more; in labours more abundant, in stripes above* *measure, in prisons more frequent, in deaths oft. Of the Jews five times received I forty stripes save one. Thrice was I beaten with rods, once was I stoned, thrice I suffered shipwreck, a night and a day I have been in the deep; In journeyings often, in perils of waters, in perils of robbers, in perils by mine own countrymen, in perils by the heathen, in perils in the city, in perils in the wilderness, in perils in the sea, in perils among false brethren; In weariness and painfulness, in watchings often, in hunger and thirst, in fastings often, in cold and nakedness. Beside those things that are without, that which cometh upon me daily, the care of all the churches."*

After narrating what he had gone through, Paul concludes the portion of Scripture in **2 Corinthians 11:23 - 28** by saying *"...Beside those things that are without, that which cometh upon me daily, the care of all the churches"*

His deepest desire and concern was for the churches. He had no other agenda in ministry but to ensure that the Kingdom of God expands and the churches excelled in their calling. This is a high manifestation of a Kingdom mindset.

Apostolic Mindsets & Paradigms

Chapter Five: Apostolic Paradigm Shifts

Defining Paradigms and Paradigm Shifts

A paradigm is a standard, perspective, or set of ideas. It is a way of looking at something. It can also be viewed as a pattern, a model or a framework. At any one time in an organisation or a church, there are dominant paradigms that determine the patterns that govern that church or organisation. The church model is directly influenced by the existing paradigms.

Paradigms are also defined as beliefs, ideas, images, and verbal descriptions that are consciously or unconsciously formed from experiences. This means that paradigms are either formed deliberately or without any deliberate effort.

When paradigms are formed they guide thoughts and actions within or along certain channels. The preaching styles, the order of worship, the sitting arrangements, the type of music and the governing of the church are all products of paradigms.

A paradigm shift is a fundamental change in approach or underlying assumptions or traditions. When a paradigm shift occurs, it involves a shift from one mindset to another. Nothing can bring radical change in a person's life or an organisation more than a paradigm shift. When old traditions and strongholds are replaced by new and fresh ideas, it literally changes one's approach to life. Once in a while paradigm shifts are necessary to bring churches into alignment with the will and purposes of God.

There are certain things that were inherited from previous generations that tend to lose relevance over the years. These fall mainly into the category of human church traditions which have nothing to do with the Word of God. Whilst some traditions might have served their purpose during the time when they were implemented, it is important to underscore that the work of God is dynamic and needs not be limited by old customs or ways of doing things. God is calling the church into the apostolic paradigm. Apostolic paradigm shifts will bring the church into full alignment with God's desires for this century.

Whenever paradigm shifts begin to occur, generally the people involved tend to be uncomfortable. The discomfort is a result of having to let go what was normal and replace it with something new. When Jesus came to the earth, he dealt with a lot of old paradigms as He desired to fulfill the will of His Father on the earth. Transitions and dispensational changes are met with mixed reactions. There are those who quickly come into alignment, some who are slow to align and others who resistantly

141

change. There are also those who totally resist and reject any kind of shift. Such were the kinds of reactions that Jesus faced in His day. His teachings were formulated to break the old style of thinking and beliefs.

Matthew 5:21-27 - *"Ye have heard that it was said by them of old time, Thou shalt not kill; and whosoever shall kill shall be in danger of the judgment: But I say unto you, That whosoever is angry with his brother without a cause shall be in danger of the judgment: and whosoever shall say to his brother, Raca, shall be in danger of the council: but whosoever shall say, Thou fool, shall be in danger of hell fire. Therefore if thou bring thy gift to the altar, and there rememberest that thy brother hath ought against thee; Leave there thy gift before the altar, and go thy way; first be reconciled to thy brother, and then come and offer thy gift. Agree with thine adversary quickly, whiles thou art in the way with him; lest at any time the adversary deliver thee to the* *judge, and the judge deliver thee to the officer, and thou be cast into prison. Verily I say unto thee, Thou shalt by no means come out thence, till thou hast paid the uttermost farthing. Ye have heard that it was said by them of old time, Thou shalt not commit adultery: But I say unto you, That whosoever looketh on a woman to lust after her hath committed adultery with her already in his heart."*

Jesus in His statements above, started by quoting the old way of thinking before introducing a new way of thinking.

In **Matthew 5:21**, He says *"Ye have heard that it was said by them of old time, Thou shalt not kill; and whosoever shall kill shall be in danger of the judgment But I say unto you, That whosoever is angry with his brother without a cause shall be in danger of the judgment'.*

It is important to notice that the things people hear ultimately formulate the dominant paradigms in their minds. Jesus, because He was the Son of God, was bringing the people of God into a new dispensation of grace.

John 1:16-17 - *"And of his fullness have all we received, and grace for grace. For the law was given by Moses, but grace and truth came by Jesus Christ."*

Many questioned His authority, yet He was the Son of the Living God. Many struggled with His teachings, yet He was the Way, the Truth and the Life. Many even accused Him of using demons to do the work of healing that He was doing.

Luke 20:2 - *"And spake unto him, saying, Tell us, by what authority doest thou these things? or who is he that gave thee this authority?"*

After a few years of ministry, Jesus accomplished His mission on the earth, and all believers today continue to partake of the salvation and glory of His work. Generations have come and gone, and yet the church is still alive and progressing because of the work of our Lord and Saviour, Jesus Christ. The foundation was laid through the work of Christ. God is calling the church to continue to walk into the fullness of His will and purpose. God does not desire the church to miss His divine will and purpose. Along the way certain paradigm shifts are required so that the church continues to fulfill its mandate so as to remain relevant to all generations. There is an apostolic generation that God is raising in this time.

Paradigm Shift from Carnal to Spiritual Mindset

One of the first paradigm shifts that needs to happen in the church is the shift from carnality to spirituality. There can never be an apostolic paradigm that can take place without this shift. As long as the church remains in carnality its influence and impact will be minimal. The word carnal means **'fleshly, bodily, sensuous and lascivious'.**

The Bible speaks of two main types of mindsets that can exist in the church. These mindsets determine a lot as far as the destiny of the church is concerned. To live a successful and victorious Christian lives, it is important to take note of these two mindsets.

Proverbs 23:7 - *"For as he thinketh in his heart, so is he..."*

Romans 8:6 - *"For to be carnally minded is death; but to be spiritually minded is life and peace."*

According to **Romans 8:6** above, there are two mindsets that can be operational in individuals or churches. These two are:

1. The Carnal Mindset – This is Lower Nature (Sensuous) Paradigm. It is a paradigm that feeds on carnality and is inclined towards fleshly and earthly things.

2. The Spiritual Mindset – This is the Higher Apostolic Paradigm that is exhibited by mature individuals and churches.

At any one moment, a church can either be governed by The Carnal Mindset (The Lower Nature Paradigm) or The Spiritual Mindset (Higher Apostolic Paradigm).

As noted already, the first paradigm shift that needs to happen in the church is the shift from a carnal mindset to a spiritual mindset. Unless this happens, the church will operate at a very low level in all its functions. There is need to check and deal with paradigms that are dominant in the church so as to align with God and move towards a glorious destiny.

The Limitations of a Carnal Mindset

In the Bible, the church at Corinth demonstrated carnality at the highest level. They were endowed with many spiritual gifts but very carnal in their conduct e.g. getting drunk during Holy Communion, a person sleeping with his mother, fighting and quarrelling amongst themselves and different kinds of divisions. There are many limitations that manifest when a carnal mindset is operational in a church.

1. Carnal mindset is limited in scope.
The scope of a carnal mindset is extremely limited. It is a narrow and shallow mindset. This is because the scope of the carnal mindset is limited to fleshly things. People with a carnal

mind cannot think beyond the physical realm. Carnal churches limit themselves to fleshly or physical realm only.

1 Corinthians 3:4 - *"For while one saith, I am of Paul; and another, I am of Apollos; are ye not carnal?"*

The church at Corinth was limited in scope because of carnality which was dominant. Carnal people are always sowing fleshly seeds.

Galatians 6:8 – *"For he that soweth to his flesh shall of the flesh reap corruption..."*

The scope of a carnal person is to please the flesh. Carnal people continuously struggle with issues of the flesh. The ultimate result of remaining in carnality is corruption and death.

Romans 8:6-8 - *"For to be carnally minded is death; but to be spiritually minded is life and*

149

peace. Because the carnal mind is enmity against God: for it is not subject to the law of God, neither indeed can be. So then they that are in the flesh cannot please God."

A carnal mindset also delights in factionalism and finds comfort in a special group. There are people who find joy and amusement in fights, factions and divisions.

1 Corinthians 3:4 - *"For while one saith, I am of Paul; and another, I am of Apollos; are ye not carnal?"*

I have often seen a number of believers who never really want to work with others within the church. They find delight in belonging to a faction or a clique. This becomes a serious challenge when it happens in the church. Great leaders swiftly address and break factionalism because it limits and derails the progress of the church.

A carnal mindset also delights in competition. There are some people who are extremely competitive in their approach towards God's work and life in general. They manifest the spirit of competition in everything that they do. Such people always desire to outdo others so that they appear to be the best. I once worked with a lady who was obsessed with the spirit of competition. She would always go out of her way because of a desire to remain at the top. Her life was followed with many stresses and strains because she could not cope with such a lifestyle. She often got into serious depression because of her obsession to have the best car, the best house, the latest style of clothes and the best life. This was a manifestation of carnality at its height. In life there will always be people with better things and there is no way one person can have the best of everything.

This is quite sad because there are ministers and ministries that also get into the carnal mode. Such ministers and ministries never really go far because their motives are not pure. God can never really bless anyone whose motives are not pure.

1 Corinthians 3:1 - *"And I, brethren, could not speak unto you as unto spiritual, but as unto carnal, even as unto babes in Christ."*

Carnal people are limited in scope and capacity. Their minds cannot think broadly. They think about the NOW only. Like babies, they cannot carry the deep things of God. At times people fail to progress and fulfill their destinies because of the limited scope that comes with carnality. The failure to receive revelation, the anointing and God's blessing is tied to carnality.

1 Corinthians 2:14 - *"But the natural man receiveth not the things of the Spirit of God: for they are foolishness unto him: neither can he* *know them, because they are spiritually discerned."*

A church that remains in the state of carnality will never be able to step into the apostolic paradigm.

2. Carnal mindset is limited in understanding.

A carnal mindset is also limited in understanding. People who are carnal reason like babies. There comes a time when the church needs to move from infancy to maturity.

1 Corinthians 14:20 - *"Brethren, be not children in understanding: howbeit in malice be ye children, but in understanding be men."*

It is very difficult to knock sense into carnal people. No matter how much you explain certain truths to some people, they never seem to get it. Churches which are generally carnal always fail to embrace certain truths because of limitations in understanding.

Ephesians 5:17 - *"Wherefore be ye not unwise, but understanding what the will of the Lord is..."*

They lack understanding in divine things and the will of God. As a result, they walk in disobedience and often go against the Word of God.

Romans 1:31 - *"Without understanding, covenant breakers, without natural affection, implacable, unmerciful..."*

Many times people struggle to do what God commands in his Word because of a lack of understanding. Paul describes his understanding when he was still a child in the Book of 1 Corinthians 13:11.

1 Corinthians 13:11 - *"When I was a child, I spake as a child, I understood as a child, I thought as a child: but when I became a man, I put away childish things."*

When understanding is limited, the church will fail to rise up into its apostolic calling and vision. Apostolic people are those that have developed their level of understanding.

3. Carnal mindset is limited in Vision.
Carnal people only live for today, they cannot cast their vision afar. Carnality is a killer of destiny. There are some churches which seem to focus largely on temporary things instead of creating an environment for longevity.

Hebrews 12:16 - *"Lest there be any fornicator, or profane person, as Esau, who for one morsel of meat sold his birthright."*

Numbers 13:33 - *"And there we saw the giants, the sons of Anak, which come of the giants: and we were in our own sight as grasshoppers, and so we were in their sight."*

Some of the spies who went into the land of promise did not have a vision that they could inherit the land. They came back with an evil report and thought that it was an impossible task. Carnality cannot see possibilities but always sees impossibilities.

Numbers 13:32 - *"And they brought up an evil report of the land which they had searched unto the children of Israel, saying, The land, through which we have gone to search it, is a land that eats up the inhabitants thereof; and all the people that we saw in it are men of a great stature."*

Many great destinies are destroyed because of carnality. The church cannot make it in destiny if it remains in carnality.

4. Carnal mindset is limited relationally

People who are carnally minded also struggle to relate well with God and others because of the limited depth. They cannot see far or deep enough.

Romans 8:7 - *"Because the carnal mind is enmity against God: for it is not subject to the law of God, neither indeed can be."*

If carnality dominates a church, the level of prayer, worship and fasting is very limited as well. Generally many people in the church also struggle to embrace and follow the word of God. There are people who have been in the church for a very long time but still struggle with simple principles like giving, tithing, fasting and worship. People with carnal mindsets also struggle to relate well with others. This was the case with the church at Corinth.

1 Corinthians 3:3 - *"For ye are yet carnal: for whereas there is among you envying, and strife, and divisions, are ye not carnal, and walk as men?"*

Carnal people struggle in relating with fellow saints. I have encountered believers who are socially impaired because of carnality. They are so arrogant that they cannot have a normal conversation with anyone. They often cause strife and divisions among people and as a result create confusion among people. One of the greatest marks of maturity is how people in the church relate with others.

Apostolic paradigms demand people who are relationally mature because the apostolic requires a lot of networking. It is the ability to network with different kinds of people that distinguishes apostolic people from non-apostolic people. The ability to relate with people from all backgrounds is one of the greatest signs of maturity in the things of God.

5. Carnal mindset is limited in faith.

Carnal people cannot rise beyond a certain level of faith. A carnal mindset cripples faith in a person's life. Carnal people often fail to believe God for simple things. A church which remains in carnality will not raise its faith to believe God for great things. On the contrary such a church is full of people who are pessimistic and negative. It is a great pain for any leader to lead people who are negative concerning the vision. Carnal people always struggle in their faith walk, and fail to rise above their circumstances.

1 Corinthians 5:2 - *"And ye are puffed up, and have not rather mourned, that he that hath done this deed might be taken away from among you. For I verily, as absent in body, but present in* *spirit, have judged already, as though I were present, concerning him that hath so done this deed."*

Carnal people lack the ability to judge things properly. They may rejoice where there is need for mourning, or start mourning where there is need to rejoice. This is because carnality negatively affects the faith of the believers.

The Power of a Spiritual Mindset

All great men who accomplished great things in Scriptures were spiritual. They could see beyond what carnal people could see.

1. It is a Visionary Mindset

The spiritual mindset is visionary in nature. A spiritual church is driven by vision. Abraham became the father of faith because he was a spiritual man. Abraham responded to God even when he did not know the full details of God's plan. A church that is spiritual always takes steps of faith towards God's direction.

Hebrews 11:8 - *"By faith Abraham, when he was called to go out into a place which he should after receive for an inheritance, obeyed; and he went out, not knowing whither he went."*

Abraham maintained his faith and relationship with God despite the challenges that he went through.

Romans 4:20-23 – *"He staggered not at the promise of God through unbelief; but was strong in faith, giving glory to God; and being fully persuaded that, what he had promised, he was able also to perform. And therefore it was imputed to him for righteousness."*

When God challenged Abraham to sacrifice his son, Abraham responded almost instantly. Any church that desires to walk in this higher

161

paradigm should be prepared to follow the instructions of God at any moment. There are some ministers and ministries that do not bother to listen to what God is saying. In such a case, there is no sense of direction or vision that exists in the church.

Genesis 22:2-3 - *"And he said, Take now thy son, thine only son Isaac, whom thou lovest, and get thee into the land of Moriah; and offer him there for a burnt offering upon one of the mountains which I will tell thee of.And Abraham rose up early in the morning, and saddled his ass, and took two of his young men with him, and Isaac his son, and clave the wood for the burnt offering, and rose up, and went unto the place of which God had told him."*

A church will not advance much if it ignores the voice of God or the promptings of the Spirit. Leaders and ministers should learn to declare what God is saying over the church in different seasons. The church should have a sense of direction. The voice of God spoke in response to Abraham's obedience to God's voice.

Genesis 22:11-12 - *"And the angel of the LORD called unto him out of heaven, and said, Abraham, Abraham: and he said, Heream I. And he said, Lay not thine hand upon the lad, neither do thou any thing unto him: for now I know that thou fearest God, seeing thou hast not withheld thy son, thine only son from me."*

God honored Abraham because he was spiritually minded and oriented. The church needs to be spiritually oriented.

2. It is a Discerning Mindset.
The spiritual mindset is a highly discerning mindset. People who are spiritual are generally discerning people. The apostolic paradigm calls for the church to be discerning. The ability to discern means the church is sharp and can

discriminate and distinguish between purity vs. evil, error vs. truth as well as the Spirit of God vs. other kinds of spirits.

Joseph was very discerning because he had a spiritual mindset. His ability to interpret dreams demonstrated his discerning capability. Leaders need to interpret the happenings in the environment. Unless the church rises up as an interpreter of the times in cities and nations, the future will be gloomy. The interpretation of Joseph literally changed an entire nation. The land was saved from a devastating famine because of an interpreter in the form of Joseph.

Genesis 41:39-40 - *"And Pharaoh said unto Joseph, Forasmuch as God hath shewed thee all this, there is none so discreet and wise as thou art: Thou shalt be over my house, and according unto thy word shall all my people be ruled: only in the throne will I be greater than thou."*

Daniel rose up to be a prominent apostolic leader in Babylon because of spirituality and a discerning mindset. God revealed secrets to Daniel because of his spiritual stance. He was a man given to prayer and seeking the face of God. Daniel was very consistent in his prayer life and relationship with God.

Daniel 2:19 - *"Then was the secret revealed unto Daniel in a night vision. Then Daniel blessed the God of heaven."*

Daniel 6:10 - *"Now when Daniel knew that the writing was signed, he went into his house; and his windows being open in his chamber toward Jerusalem, he kneeled upon his knees three times a day, and prayed, and gave thanks before his God, as he did aforetime."*

A lot of people have walked into deception and error because of the absence of a discerning mindset. There are many things that appear to be godly on the surface and yet there is a wrong spirit behind them. Any great apostolic church should deal with false doctrines and deceptive spirits. Globally, there has been a rise of ministers and false prophets who use other kinds of spirits which are not of God. The use of marine (water) spirits has become very common by ministers who seek personal fame and glory. It is only apostolic people and churches who can discern and bring down such strongholds.

Matthew 7:21-23 - *"Not every one that saith unto me, Lord, Lord, shall enter into the kingdom of heaven; but he that doeth the will of my Father which is in heaven. Many will say to me in that day, Lord, Lord, have we not prophesied in thy name? and in thy name have cast out devils? and in thy name done many wonderful works? And then will I profess unto them, I never knew you: depart from me, ye that work iniquity."*

3. It is a Renewed Mindset

A renewed mindset does not conform to the world standards but to the standards of God's Word.

Romans 12:2 - *"And be not conformed to this world: but be ye transformed by the renewing of your mind, that ye may prove what is that good, and acceptable, and perfect, will of God."*

It is absolutely important for the church to be renewed in the mind. The mind needs to be aligned more and more to God's will and standards. An apostolic paradigm shift involves the process of the renewing of the mind. The minds of the people can be renewed through strong apostolic doctrinal teachings. The Apostles in the Book of Acts were steadfast in the apostolic doctrine.

Acts 2:42 - *"And they continued stedfastly in the apostles' doctrine and fellowship, and in breaking of bread, and in prayers."*

The doctrine is one of the greatest weapons that can renew the mind. When there is a constant supply of sound doctrine in the church, people's minds get renewed. The word has power to bring transformation to the church in an amazing way. The Bible in the book of Ephesians speaks of the washing of water with the word.

Ephesians 5:25-27 - *"Husbands, love your wives, even as Christ also loved the church, and gave himself for it; That he might sanctify and cleanse it with the washing of water by the word, That he might present it to himself a glorious church, not having spot, or wrinkle, or any such thing; but that it should be holy and without blemish."*

The challenge happens when the church continues in an unrenewed state of mind. This creates a scenario where the church is governed by worldly standards. That is why there are believers and churches who are comfortable using worldly products and worldly people as part of their desire to grow and get fame. There are some who play worldly music comfortably whilst some allow worldly superstars to teach the saints from their pulpits. The Bible clearly states that whilst we are in this world but we are not of this world. This simply means that the world cannot dictate how the church should function.

John 15:19 - *"If ye were of the world, the world would love his own: but because ye are not of the world, but I have chosen you out of the world, therefore the world hateth you."*

1 John 2:15 – *"Love not the world, neither the things that are in the world. If any man loves the world, the love of the Father is not in him."*

Whilst the church has got the obligation to reach out to the world with the Gospel, it appears there are churches which are bringing worldly patterns into their churches so as to increase their popularity ratings. This is surely not the order of God. The order of God is that church should present the Gospel to the world so that men and women may be saved. Apostolic churches and leaders have the power and capacity to bring down worldly systems and establish the order of the Kingdom of God.

Daniel was one apostolic leader that had a strong renewed mindset which caused him not to defile himself. He kept himself from the contamination of the Babylonian systems. He demonstrated spiritual maturity that caused him to be lifted up in that land.

Daniel 1:8 - *"But Daniel purposed in his heart that he would not defile himself with the portion of the king's meat, nor with the wine which he drank: therefore he requested of the prince of the eunuchs that he might not defile himself."*

The church should keep itself from all forms of worldly contamination. Job became the greatest man in the East because he was a spiritual man with a renewed mind. He continued to fear God and remained spiritual despite the challenges that he faced.

Job 1:1 - *"There was a man in the land of Uz, whose name was Job; and that man was perfect and upright, and one that feared God, and eschewed evil."*

Job 42:12 - *"So the LORD blessed the latter end of Job more than his beginning: for he had fourteen thousand sheep, and six thousand* *camels, and a thousand yoke of oxen, and a thousand she asses."*

There are many challenges that the church will have to deal with by virtue of it being surrounded by worldly systems. However, it is important that the church remains focused and steadfast in the ways and principles of God.

4. It is a Steadfast Mindset

The spiritual mindset is also a steadfast mindset. Spiritual minded people are not easily moved because of their steadfastness. The Apostolic paradigm calls for those that are steadfast in their approach.

Isaiah 26:3 - *"Thou wilt keep him in perfect peace, whose mind is stayed on thee: because he trusteth in thee."*

Ministry work requires steady people who do not flip flop. The ability to remain steadfast overtime is one of the greatest qualities of apostolic leaders. God desires leaders who have stability in their approach to ministry. Steadfastness also implies focus. The word focus means to pay particular attention to, or the act of concentrating interest or activity on something.

One of the greatest keys for success in life is 'focus'. You can be successful at anything in life by learning how to get focused and remain focused. Focus will help anyone to go faster and further in life. Unfortunately we are living in a society that offers many things and options and as a result many people fail to focus on specific things. It is easy to be beclouded by many issues and responsibilities such that one fails to focus on anything.

There are many people who are doing many things without focusing or paying attention to what they are doing. As a result, these become ineffective because they gave very little attention to what they were doing. But those who are consistent and steadfast will go very far in life.

5. It is the Mind of Christ

Philippians 2:5 - *"...have this mind in you which was also in Christ Jesus"*

I Corinthians 2:16 - *"...but we have the mind of Christ"*

The Spiritual Mindset is also the mind of Christ. The Bible talks about the mind of Christ. Paul emphasizes in the book of Philippians that the church should have the mind of Christ. Having the mind of Christ implies two things. Firstly, it implies that the church should have the same attitude and approach that Christ had. Christ had a mind which was focused on the Father. Christ had a

174

mind of accomplishing the work of salvation. Christ had a mind of doing the will of God. For the church to succeed it should also have the same mind.

To have the mind of Christ also implies tapping into the spirit realm so as to understand the mind of God at a particular point in time. The church needs to see things from God's perspective. An apostolic church is one that taps into the mind of God to get vision and direction. In every season God is always communicating something to His church and to His people. If the church misses the mind of God it begins to operate in the lower paradigm of carnality. It is very easy for the church to deviate from the mind of God to a place of operating in the flesh.

For that reason, every apostolic church should cultivate an atmosphere for the Presence of God as well as the prophetic. When the Spirit of God moves in the church, it is easy to hear the voice of God. The apostolic leaders of Antioch were praying and ministering unto the Lord when the Holy Spirit spoke concerning Barnabas and Saul (Paul).

Acts 13:2-4 - *"As they ministered to the Lord, and fasted, the Holy Ghost said, Separate me Barnabas and Saul for the work whereunto I have called them. And when they had fasted and prayed, and laid their hands on them, they sent them away. So they, being sent forth by the Holy Ghost, departed unto Seleucia; and from thence they sailed to Cyprus."*

Churches should be steadfast to maintain the culture of prayer, fasting, praise and worship. This way, the mind of Christ can prevail in the church. The church begins to think like Christ.

Acts 4:31 - *"And when they had prayed, the place was shaken where they were assembled* *together; and they were all filled with the Holy Ghost, and they spake the word of God with boldness."*

Once the church taps into this paradigm, there is great progress that begins to happen. A lot of churches are hampered in their progress because they do not tap into the mind of God. God has a desire to lift up every church, but unfortunately some leaders are too busy to tap into the mind of God. Ministers should never be too busy to tap into the mind of God.

Caleb was one man who tapped into the mind of God when all the other spies thought it was an impossible task. For this reason Caleb had a progressive mindset that caused him to be blessed of the Lord.

Numbers 13:30 - *"And Caleb stilled the people before Moses, and said, Let us go up at once,* *and possess it; for we are well able to overcome it."*

The spies represent some leaders in the church who cannot perceive what God is saying or doing. I have seen a number of church elders who give their own Pastors problems because of carnality. When a Pastor is surrounded by elders who cannot perceive or tap into the mind of God, there are struggles and scuffles that begin to take place. This is a very unfortunate scenario because ministry work is for people who are sensitive to the moves of God. If all ministry decisions are made from a purely natural standpoint, the church will not go anywhere. There are moments where God demands people of faith who can perceive and see into the future. There are some who are very strict on budgets and human made plans and they do not allow any room for God's hand and provision. In the ministry, there are some things that need to be done by faith without full knowledge of what lies ahead. This is not to advocate that leaders should be irrational and irresponsible, but they should be sensitive to God's direction. This takes spiritual maturity and divine wisdom.

God honored Caleb eventually because he was a spiritual man. He had a clear apostolic mindset and paradigm that was working in him.

Numbers 14:24 - *"But my servant Caleb, because he had another spirit with him, and hath followed me fully, him will I bring into the land where into he went; and his seed shall possess it."*

People who operate within an apostolic paradigm believe that all things are possible. This is when the church takes on the mind of Christ.

Apostolic Mindsets & Paradigms

Chapter Six: Paradigm Shifts for Apostolic Churches & Leaders

As noted in the previous chapter, a paradigm shift occurs when a person or an organisation has an epitome that is so profound that it forever changes the way the person or the organisation perceives and reacts to a certain set of circumstances or more importantly a certain belief system.

The Importance of Paradigm Shifts

Paradigm shifts are critical for leaders and churches for a number of reasons. Firstly, what people see (or perceive) determines how they feel and how they feel determines their actions (what they do). Actions are therefore a product of existing and dominant paradigms. Paradigm shifts are therefore the only path through which people and organisations can change and improve overtime. Without paradigm shifts people would continue to walk along the same path even though in some cases the path may be harmful.

Secondly some churches and organisations have lost relevance overtime because they have remained static in their approach and thinking. The world is very dynamic and as the world changes, each period in history often brings new challenges. The only way to deal and address those challenges is through paradigm shifts. The Word of God remains the same but it has to be applied in a relevant way in all generations. This can only happen if leaders and churches go through paradigm shifts. This way the church will remain relevant in addressing the issues that affect people and communities.

Thirdly, God often reveals truths from His Word that need to be emphasized in different generations. It is therefore important for the church to remain sensitive to God and preach the 'message of the hour' or the current message that God will be stressing. It does not help to preach a yester year message if God is saying something else today. God is always saying something to every new generation that emerges. Paradigm shifts are therefore, essential to ensure that what is in the heart of God is released to the church. Apostolic leaders always carry a timely message that is in line with the purposes of God.

Apostolic Paradigm Shifts for Churches

We are living in a highly sophisticated time as leaders and ministers of the Gospel. This has been dubbed the 'Information Age' where our churches and congregants are highly exposed to information on many technological platforms such as the internet and social media. Ministers therefore cannot afford to be ignorant in terms of knowing the latest and current trends that are happening across the different spheres of life. Long back it was easy for ministers to say and preach things without anyone questioning the integrity of the Word, but because of the exposure that people now have, it is important for ministers to be sound and be on top of their game.

It is therefore, important for leaders to go through paradigm shifts in ministry so as to remain relevant. The following are some of the key paradigm shifts that are required by ministers:

1. A shift from a common church model to an apostolic church model

The first apostolic paradigm shift that is required in a church is to move from the common church model to the apostolic church model. The church has to position itself apostolically. There is need to understand the apostolic model and to develop an apostolic flair in ministry. The Apostolic Model is key in building influential and dominant churches that have a territorial impact.

Pastors and leaders should understand that the church entity is not just a place for inward healing and ministry, but the church is positioned by God for territorial influence. Not only should the church be a place where people can gather to worship and be refreshed, but it should be a place where apostolic strategies and goals are set, as believers are equipped, activated and released into ministry. This approach and paradigm will shift the attention of the church from being just inward looking to a place where the church begins to find ways of impacting societies, cities and nations.

In a case where one ministry has a number of churches in a region, the network of churches can build a strong apostolic hub. There is power in such a network because as churches grow and increase, the apostolic hub also increases in its influence. The individual churches within the network can also mature overtime and become apostolic centers in their own right as well.

It is therefore important for leaders and church members to view their churches not just as ordinary local churches but apostolic centers that are positioned to influence entire communities, towns and cities. This apostolic paradigm shift will create great room for amazing levels of growth and expansion. This shift will also cause enlargement and an increase in the apostolic anointing.

With this paradigm shift, apostolic churches will be able to do the following things:

a) **Plant New Works and/or Churches.**

New churches, new home groups, new ministries and new works become the order of the day when the church embraces the apostolic paradigm. Anyone that operates by the apostolic paradigm is wired or programmed to see the birth new works.

b)   Train and raise leaders.

This paradigm will also cause the church to get into the mode of training and raising leaders. An awareness of the greatness and the intensity of the apostolic work suddenly causes the church to have no option but to develop people that can carry the apostolic vision forward.

c)   Ordain and release leaders.

The training and nurturing of new leaders will culminate into the ordination and release of these leaders. Ordination can take place as leaders are set apart into different kinds of ministerial offices e.g. pastoral work, eldership or evangelism. It is unfortunate that there are some leaders who do not place importance in ordination. As a result there are several individuals who operate as Pastors and Elders without being ordained by anyone. This is a very dangerous way of functioning in ministry.

The biblical order is for God's servants to be properly set apart and ordained for ministry work. Once leaders have been set apart, they can be released to fully function in their ministerial offices. Barnabas and Saul (Paul) were released by the apostolic leaders at Antioch.

Acts 13:1-3 - *"Now there were in the church that was at Antioch certain prophets and teachers; as Barnabas, and Simeon that was called Niger, and Lucius of Cyrene, and Manaen, which had been brought up with Herod the tetrarch, and Saul. As they ministered to the Lord, and fasted, the Holy Ghost said, Separate me Barnabas and Saul for the work whereunto I have called them. And when they had fasted and prayed, and laid their hands on them, they sent them away."*

d)   Influence cities and communities.

Communities, cities and nations can easily be influenced by an apostolic church. Apostolic churches have a great appetite to spread the Gospel everywhere. This paradigm then causes the church to invariably grow in its influence. In the Bible, we notice that Paul and Silas were noted as men who had turned the world upside-down. Such is the level of influence that God desires to bring upon churches.

Acts 17:4-6 - *"And some of them believed, and consorted with Paul and Silas; and of the devout Greeks a great multitude, and of the chief women not a few. But the Jews which believed not, moved with envy, took unto them certain lewd fellows of the baser sort, and gathered a company, and set all the city on an uproar, and assaulted the house of Jason, and sought to bring them out to the people. And when they found them not, they drew Jason and certain brethren unto the rulers of the city, crying, These that have turned the world upside down are come hither also."*

e)   Increase in signs and wonders.

There is a corresponding increase in signs and wonders that takes place when the church hooks onto an apostolic paradigm. When the church takes on an aggressive apostolic mode, the heavens are opened and signs and wonders become the order of the day. In the Book of Acts, there was a manifestation of many great signs and wonders because the church was highly apostolic.

Acts 5:12 - *"And by the hands of the apostles were many signs and wonders wrought among the people; (and they were all with one accord in Solomon's porch."*

An apostolic church is a church on a mission. Apostolic churches are driven by the desire to fulfil the Great Commission. This is why such apostolic churches are followed by great signs and wonders. Anytime the church aligns with the heartbeat of God there is a release of great signs and wonders. Therefore there is need for a major shift in the church from an inward focus only to an outward focus of ministry.

2. A shift from a self-centered model to a reproduction model

The second apostolic paradigm shift is the transition from a self-centered model approach to a reproduction model approach. Reproduction is the action or process of copying, replicating or duplicating something. Usually something that is reproduced takes the form or has the resemblance of the original. It is a close imitation of the original. The apostolic paradigm triggers the desire to reproduce. As a result, apostolic churches ensure that there is continuity by raising faithful sons, imparting and replicating the anointing as well as releasing the DNA, or the spiritual genes to the people.

The Apostle Paul encouraged the church at Corinth to follow the pattern and lifestyle that he had demonstrated to them.

1 Corinthians 11:1 - *"Be ye followers of me, even as I also am of Christ."*

This process of reproduction is a crucial process that guarantees that the apostolic work continues to grow. Many churches cease to grow because they do not have a reproduction model. Paul had imparted something upon Timothy and he also encouraged Timothy do to likewise.

2 Timothy 2:2 - *"And the things that thou hast heard of me among many witnesses, the same commit thou to faithful men, who shall be able to teach others also."*

There is need to impart the anointing, gifts, teachings and graces to faithful people in the church. The days of one man band (superstar) churches are over. The vision should be spread and carried by the corporate body. Old paradigms focus on having a single superstar leader but new paradigms focus on creating a culture of leadership. The culture of leadership should be cultivated in churches so as to produce as many sons and leaders as possible. There is a great need to perpetuate the spirit of sonship and leadership. This means that leaders need to invest people so as to develop them.

A true apostolic paradigm is one that has the following dimensions:

a)   Gathering Dimension

Leaders and church members should be gathered often besides the usual Sunday services to ensure there is impartation that takes place. This way, spiritual genes are transferred from fathers to sons. All types of gatherings should result in impartation, the transfer of the anointing, the release of the vision and spirit of the house.

b)   Teaching Dimension

Teaching ensures that the saints are equipped with sound apostolic doctrine. Once apostolic doctrine has been imparted to the church, it is easy for the church to carry the apostolic spirit.

c)   Equipping Dimension

Apostolic equipping is the process of preparing, training and arming the church for ministerial work. Tried and tested sons should be equipped with tools and resources that allow them to spread the vision. This entails that much training has to be done within churches. Training is one of the best ways to equip those that will eventually be released into ministry.

d)   Assigning Dimension

Apostolic assignments should become the order of the day in churches. Apostolic assignments are simple ministerial tasks that are given to the people by the leaders with the purpose of increasing the capacity of the church. The passing or failure of apostolic assignments distinguishes between false and genuine sons. The more the apostolic assignments that are given to church members, the quicker they grow to become apostolic leaders in their own right. Teams of people may also be deployed with specific mandates so as to spread the vision. Leaders should also travel and work with teams so that they can catch the vision.

e)   Discipleship Dimension
There is also need to run discipleship and training programs. There is need for new converts to go through discipleship so that they can grow from being mere infants to the place where they fully mature. Jesus commissioned the church to make disciples.

f)   Target Dimension

Every church that desires to be apostolic should be target oriented. Churches should work with targets that they aim to get to. These targets can be places earmarked for planting new works, new leaders that need to be raised, number of souls to be won or even growth targets for the church. An apostolic paradigm demands that the church looks at its surroundings and target specific places to influence.

g)   Building Dimension

The building of the church should continue in all ages and generations until Jesus comes. The church is a spiritual house that should continuously be built so that it becomes more and more glorious.

1 Peter 2:5 - *"Ye also, as lively stones, are built up a spiritual house, an holy priesthood, to offer up spiritual sacrifices, acceptable to God by Jesus Christ."*

1 Corinthians 3:10 - *"According to the grace of God which is given unto me, as a wise masterbuilder, I have laid the foundation, and another buildeth thereon. But let every man take heed how he buildeth thereupon."*

All these elements above will result in the reproduction and increase in the church.

3. A shift from a theoretical model to a practical demonstration model

People often get tired of theories hence it is absolutely critical for leaders and churches to walk the talk. The message that is carried and preached should be followed by a practical demonstration of the same message in the lives of ministers and leaders. Leaders cannot preach what they do not believe in or what they do not practice. Modern ministers and the church are now being thoroughly scrutinized by the world in general and any deviation from the values that the minister or church preaches is questioned.

Apostolic leaders and churches should have evidence of the things that they declare. Some unbelievers have been hindered from coming to church because they see no difference between themselves and the Christians. The church needs to move to the paradigm where it truly becomes the light and beacon to the rest of the world. Jesus describes this church as a city that is set on a hill.

Matthew 5:14 - *"Ye are the light of the world. A city that is set on a hill cannot be hid."*

This Scripture above implies a practical church that demonstrates the power of the Gospel of Christ. Pastors and leaders should not just teach healing, but they should pray and lay hands on the sick for healing. Preachers should not just teach deliverance, but demonic spirits should be cast out and dealt with. Leaders should not just talk about giving and tithing, but they should demonstrate giving by being among the highest givers in their churches. The preaching of the Word should always be followed by evidence and confirmation for it to be effective.

Mark 16:20 - *"And they went forth, and preached everywhere, the Lord working with them, and confirming the word with signs following. Amen."*

Some Pastors are hesitant to flow and move in the Spirit. This limits the levels and dimensions of the power of God that is released in the church. An apostolic church should allow the move of the Holy Spirit, the gifts of the Holy Spirit and the power of God to flow. It is not enough for the church to declare the word without corresponding action that triggers the release of the anointing. After preaching a message on the Baptism of the Holy Spirit, a minister should be bold enough to pray for people that need to be filled with the Holy Spirit. After preaching a message on revival, let there be prayer for revival and an atmosphere that triggers revival in the church.

When this happens, the church begins to experience new levels of grace and the anointing. This is an important paradigm that will bring the church to the full manifestation of the glory of God. The end time church is a glorious church. The Psalmist declares that glorious things will be spoken about the church.

Psalm 87:3 - *"Glorious things are spoken of thee, O city of God. Selah."*

Haggai 2:9 – *"The glory of this latter house shall be greater than of the former, saith the LORD of hosts: and in this place will I give peace, saith the LORD of hosts."*

Haggai declares that the glory of the latter house will be greater than that of the former.

This means that the levels of glory in the church should always be on the increase. This can only happen when churches move from a theoretical paradigm of ministry to a demonstration type of paradigm.

Ministers should also apply the Word of God consistently in their lives. I know of people who have a tendency of theorizing the Gospel. They have no firsthand experience of ministry but they tend to be very vocal on issues that they do not have a clue on. Some of them are even bold enough to criticize their leaders without any prior experience to real ministry. This does not help. Leaders, ministers, pastors and churches should become more practical so that they can have greater influence.

4. A shift from an unstructured model to a structured organizational model.

Structure is a very critical thing in modern ministry. There is need for churches to build a structured church with solid pillars. Without structure, the church will not get very far. From the onset, churches should endeavor to set up structures and systems that will sustain the church in the long run. Whilst the church is the Body of Christ, it runs and functions daily like any other organisation. Old paradigms tended to run away from proper structures and order of ministry, but churches cannot survive for long in the modern day without proper administration structures in place.

No matter how anointed and gifted leaders and churches may become, it is the structures of the church that will allow that anointing to keep flowing for long. There is an interesting story of a widow woman in the book of Kings. The woman was stranded financially and the prophet Elisha performed a miracle in her life that produced plenty of oil. But it is important to note that this miracle required that the woman looks for vessels in which the oil would be stored. There was no way this miracle could have happened without these vessels. These vessels represent systems and structures in the church.

The desire of God is to release His oil (anointing) and power upon the church, but certain churches are not ready because they do not have sufficient vessels (solid supporting structures). The problem is that if God releases much of His anointing upon a church that has no structures, there are bound to be problems that result from the aftermaths of the outpouring of God's anointing. If there are no leadership structures to support a revival, no counselors to deal with those that are delivered from demons, no people to follow up on new converts and no financial systems to deal with tithes and offerings that are received in the church, there are bound to be abuses and extremes that affect the ministry. This will cripple the church in the long run because the church will fail to cope with the pressures of ministry.

2 Kings 4:1-6 - *"Now there cried a certain woman of the wives of the sons of the prophets unto Elisha, saying, Thy servant my husband is dead; and thou knowest that thy servant did fear the LORD: and the creditor is come to take unto him my two sons to be bondmen. And Elisha said unto her, What shall I do for thee? tell me, what hast thou in the house? And she said, Thine handmaid hath not anything in the house, save a pot of oil. Then he said, Go, borrow thee vessels abroad of all thy neighbours, even empty vessels; borrow not a few. And when thou art come in, thou shalt shut the door upon thee and upon thy sons, and shalt pour out into all those vessels, and thou shalt set aside that which is full. So she went from him, and shut the door upon her and upon her sons, who brought the vessels to her; and she poured out. And it came to pass, when the vessels were full, that she said unto her son, Bring me yet a vessel. And he said unto her, There is not a vessel more. And the oil stayed."*

I was once told of a story of a Pastor who used to take offering money after every Sunday service. He would take the offering basket and buy groceries after every service. He would pay for his groceries straight from the offering basket. There was no banking or financial accountability whatsoever in his church. Such lack of discipline will only serve to cripple the church.

It is critical to have solid systems and structures in place in a church. These structures can be Financial Accounting Systems, Human Resources Systems (HR), Leadership Structures, Information and Communications Technology (ICT) Systems and Policies and Church Constitutions and Policies. As the church begins to grow and expand, these systems and structures will become very important to ensure that the church as an organisation runs smoothly. The church globally is now being challenged to account for its wellbeing and progress by governing authorities it is therefore crucial to have all structures in place. There is also need to measure things like performance in the church. This is of paramount importance as it will help to deal with non-performing leaders and entities that exist in the church.

5. A shift from a static (status quo) model to a progressive model

The final apostolic paradigm is the shift from a static (status quo) model to a progressive model. There is a need to shift from a type of thinking where churches are worried about maintaining the status quo and not wanting to come out of their comfort zones. These are people and churches who just like going with the flow. The vehicle of ministry should always be moving and going forward. A church that fails to move forward or break to the next level attracts frustration.

Today thousands of churches have no apostolic structure in place to move people beyond a teaching or pastoring-only structure into one that sends out believers. They show no ambition whatsoever and will remain on the same spot for many years. They do not have a sense of clarity and purpose. When they begin a task they abandon it in the middle before seeing it through. Their perseverance and tolerance levels are very low to sustain any amount of pressure.

When people join a church or a ministry, they can feel from the atmosphere whether the church is progressing or not. They can even tell the speed at which a church is moving. If the church remains static or too slow, the church will lose some members who are progressive in their thinking. The Bible talks of moving from faith to faith, from glory to glory and from strength to strength.

Psalm 84:7 - *"They go from strength to strength, every one of them in Zion appeareth before God."*

2 Corinthians 3:18 - *"But we all, with open face beholding as in a glass the glory of the Lord, are changed into the same image from glory to glory, even as by the Spirit of the Lord."*

Romans 1:17 - *"For therein is the righteousness of God revealed from faith to faith: as it is written, The just shall live by faith."*

The Scriptures above are pointing to the progress that should be experienced by the church. In Psalm 84:7, the psalmist addresses the church as Zion. This is a church that moves from one level of strength to another. When one looks at the church in the book of Acts, there was a hive of activity as the church continued to increase daily. In fact the Bible records that numbers were added daily to the church.

Acts 2:46 - 47 - *"And they, continuing daily with one accord in the temple, and breaking bread from house to house, did eat their meat with gladness and singleness of heart, Praising*

God, and having favour with all the people. And the Lord added to the church daily such as should be saved."

An apostolic church will keep on progressing and advancing. This is an important paradigm that churches should embrace and work with.

Characteristics of Apostolic Leadership Paradigms

1. The Apostolic Leader should be God Oriented.

Leaders are being called to come back to the place of seeking the face of God. True apostolic leaders are those that are God conscious and God oriented. This paradigm will cause leaders to have much impact. Moses, as an apostolic leader sought the face of God. He knew the ways of God.

Exodus 33:11 - *"And the LORD spake unto Moses face to face, as a man speaketh unto his* *friend. And he turned again into the camp: but his servant Joshua, the son of Nun, a young man, departed not out of the tabernacle."*

Exodus 33:18 - *"And he said, I beseech thee, shew me thy glory."*

Psalm 103:7 - *"He made known his ways unto Moses, his acts unto the children of Israel."*

2. The Apostolic Leader should be Vision Oriented

It is not enough to be called by God, but to be disciplined to follow the vision that God has given. Some people get excited about the call of God but they do not obey the demands of the call. God will demand certain things from those that he has called into the apostolic. The vision should be followed diligently by those who desire to go far in ministry.

Apostolic leaders should not be side-tracked by other things that come in the journey of ministry. It is important to keep eyes on the vision. Some start the journey very well and finish poorly. This comes as a result of side-tracking and not focusing on the vision. When a leader remains faithful to the vision, God will also show His faithfulness to that leader.

3. The Apostolic Leader should be Sacrifice Oriented

Sacrifice is something that an apostolic leader will never be able to run away from. Sacrifice has to become a lifestyle of those that desire to be used by God. The demands of ministry will certainly require lots of sacrifices. There are many kinds of sacrifices that leaders will have to make. These include career sacrifices, financial sacrifices, sacrifices of time and sacrifices of comfort.

The vision cannot go far if leaders are not willing to sacrifice. Every person that God ever used had to make some significant sacrifices in one way or the other. Some of the sacrifices are painful but they have to be done. If leaders embrace the lifestyle of sacrifice, they are bound to go far in the ministry.

4. The Apostolic Leader should be Empowerment Oriented

The apostolic ministry is about empowering others. Apostolic leaders are those who train, equip and empower those that follow after them. A genuine apostolic leader is one that leaves a legacy for his or her followers. If there is no empowerment happening in a church, then there is no progress happening there. The church only begins to move with speed if people are empowered to become solid Christians that know God and His Word.

I know of some churches were it appears that the Prophet or Leader of the church is the only one who is powerful and everyone else is a zombie that takes instructions from the leader. There have been stories that have come out in the media where congregants became victims as they were abused by men of God. This is because they were highly dependent on the man of God who never empowered them to stand on their own as believers. This is not the order of God. The New Testament Gospel is one that empowers and raises sons and leaders. Apostolic leaders work hard to empower their followers and to leave a spiritual legacy.

5. The Apostolic Leader should be People Oriented

Apostolic leaders have a heart for people and communities. They have a deep concern to meet the root needs of people. They are able to look into communities, cities and nations and work hard to improve the welfare of the people. True apostolic leaders always look at the bigger picture. They can address the manner of challenges like educational, social, economic, tribal and poverty.

6. The Apostolic Leader should be Purpose Oriented

Apostolic leaders always center on the call of God and His purpose for the Church by stirring up the people of God to become what they are capable of becoming, and to do what they are capable of doing. The purposes of God for the end time church should be fulfilled. It takes apostolic leaders who are determined to drive God's agenda and purpose in the last days. When leaders focus on purposes, the church becomes stronger.

7. The Apostolic Leader should be Kingdom Oriented

Apostolic Leaders realize that they have to work in ensuring the expansion and growth of the Kingdom of God. They have strong networks in the Body of Christ that ensure that God's mission for His kingdom is fulfilled. There has been a rise of ministers who are isolated from all other churches and ministers in the Body of

Christ. This poses a problem in the sense that it is one and the same Kingdom.

Whilst there may be variations in ministry approaches it is important for leaders to create relationships in the Body of Christ. No one church will be able to execute all the plans of God. It will take leaders and churches from across the entire Body of Christ to achieve God's agenda. Apostolic leaders are therefore those who have the Kingdom mindset that desires to see the Kingdom of God advancing forward.

Apostolic Mindsets & Paradigms

Bibliography, References & Recommended Readings

- **Apostle Colin Nyathi**, Desperate for God's Presence 2nd Edition, 2014
- **Patience S. Mupamhanga**, Women of Destiny Book 2014
- **Joyce Meyer**, Battlefield of the Mind, Devotionals 1995
- **Robert Liardon,** God's Generals, Why They Succeeded and Why Some Failed
- **Kenneth E. Hagin**, He Gave Gifts Unto Men, 1985
- **Kenneth E. Hagin**, Ministry Gifts 4th Edition, 1987
- **Derek Brown,** Transitioning in God http://rediscoveringthekingdom.info/blog/churc h-and-kingdom/transitioning-in-god-from-church-centre-to-apostolic-centre
- **Bishop Dag Heward Mills,** Loyalty And Disloyalty, 2005
- **Bishop Dag Heward Mills,** The Art of Hearing, 2006
- **Bishop Dag Heward Mills,** Fathers And Loyalty, 2011
- **Bishop David Oyedepo,** Anointing For Exploits, 2005

www.ingramcontent.com/pod-product-compliance
Lightning Source LLC
Chambersburg PA
CBHW060740050426
42449CB00008B/1279